The Hindu Tradition

The Hindu Tradition

Bithika Mukerji

AMITY HOUSE
AMITY, NEW YORK

Published by Amity House Inc.
18 High Street
Warwick, NY 10990

ISBN 0–916349–48–9

Library of Congress Catalog Card Number: 87–72991

Contents

The
Hindu
Tradition

CHAPTER ONE

WHAT IS HINDUISM?

Hinduism is the religion of the vast majority of the people of India. The language in which the source material of the religion is preserved is called *Sanskrit*, sometimes known as the language of the gods or *devabhāsā*. This divine language is distinguished from all other literary forms by virtue of its inviolate order of letters, syllables, and words, set to unique rhythms of utterance. It has been preserved in its pure form down the centuries by families of the highest priestly caste, who are required to memorize and recite the rhythms. This system forms a bulwark against errors or interpolations. The entirety of the ancient wisdom that has guided and shaped the lives of Hindus throughout the ages is called the *Vedas*. It could also be said that those who have faith in the revelatory character of the Vedas are called *Hindus.*

The term *Hinduism* has been used more as a cultural description than as a religious identification. The early Greeks and other aliens referred to the people living beyond the river Sindhu [*Hindu* to the Greeks] as *Hindus* and their religion came to be known as *Hinduism.* Hindus themselves use the word *dharma* to indicate their religion. Sometimes it is called *sanātana dharma* or "eternal religion." The word *dharma* could be construed to mean "religion," "righteousness," "duty," or "innate nature." According to Hinduism, man's innate nature is determined by a yearning for a restoration to its state of perfection. *Dharma* is the process by which the awareness of the realizable nature of perfection is enkindled in the heart of man.

The main thought, therefore, which remains constant in the varied conglomeration of ideas which constitute Hinduism is that man's nature is basically good; he is potentially capable of transcending his mortal condition and achieving the felicity of supreme bliss in this life. The wretchedness, loneliness, sorrow, and despair of human life are endemic to his human condition, but these are unnatural adjuncts and therefore to be human is to identify oneself with these alienations. Man's destiny lies in seeing himself freed from these inauthenticities.

All Hindu scriptures are nothing but voices recalling man to an understanding of this exalted state of high destiny. They speak uniformly to all men, women, and even children, in all walks of life. The spiritual dimension encompasses all aspects of life: arts and crafts, political and fiscal laws, trade customs, marital regulations, education, etc. In fact, every profession or occupation controlling life in the cities or forest hermitages is brought under the rubric of man's eternal quest for realizing God in his life. This is also the reason that all treatises and manuals dealing with the various aspects of human life are uniformly called scripture [*śāstra*]. For example, the book on dramaturgy is called *Nātyaśā-stra* and the book on economics is called *Arthaśā-stra*.

The soil of India is therefore made holy by the living presence of an unending stream of seekers after Truth and their dialogues with teachers who have attained knowledge. The one uniform format for all scriptural writings, consequently, is the dialogue. Hinduism records no sudden beginning of its history or the exploits of a founder of this faith. It may be said that there have been exemplars of the faith who have sustained it and upheld its continuity from the beginning of time. The timelessness of the Vedas is projected onto the scale of time by a galaxy of great teachers. In other words, the history of Hinduism is a history of the unfolding of the meaning of the Vedas into the "many-splendored" diversities of epics, *puranas*, "*agamas*," "*tantras*," and the sayings of saints.

Hinduism is primarily ahistorical; that is, one may understand the main principles of the religion without reference to the passing of time as history. It would be, however, a mistake to think that this body of literature is static or in danger of becoming obsolete. The texts have an inner, built-in system by which they have preserved their topicality and relevance through the ages. Since the quest is a metaphysical one and the subject of inquiry is ontology, the dialogues do not lose their significance as a result of the changes wrought by time. It is true that the context in which such questions arise is constantly undergoing transformation and in our own time is under considerable pressure from processes of alienation that seek to radicalize it.

According to Hinduism, the passing of time has a spiritual significance. Time is perceived to be characterized by the qualities of four ages as they are seen to follow one after the other in rhythmic order. The four ages are: *Satya* or the age of Truth; *Tretā* or the age when Truth loses one-fourth of its power; *Dvāpara* or the age when Truth is on the decline; and *Kali* or the age when Truth has minimal efficacy. For every age there are scriptures suited to the diminished power of the seekers of Truth. *Satya-yuga* is the age of the *Vedas; Tretā* and *Dvāpara* are guided by the *Epics, Purānas,* and *Dharmaśāstras. Āgama, Tantra,* and the utterances of saints dominate the present age of Kali. Easier modes of spiritual discipline are indicated for contemporary men and women, for when the world is of more significance than an otherworldly life of austerity *tapasya,* the quest for knowledge is so tempered by the impact of the world at the present age that even to be fully awakened to its viability is to take a step toward spiritual life.

The division of ages does not coincide with historical eras. All ages are said to be present simultaneously at all times. Yet some periods of time are marked by one predominant characteristic to the abeyance, if not the exclusion, of others. The four ages may be viewed also as a progressive order of greater concretization of the meaning of vedic statements.

The vedic message may be summarized in this verse, which belongs to one of the ancient texts:

Uttisthata jāgrata
     Prāpaya varān nibodhata
Kṣurasya dhara niśitā duratyayā
Durgam pathastat kavayo vadanti.
               Kathopanisad II.14.

(Arise! Awake! Approach the great [sages]
and learn! The wise say that the road [to
Him] is difficult to traverse as the sharp
edge of a razor

In this context, therefore, the seeker is as important as the teacher. It is to the worthy seeker that
the gracious teacher responds. Thus a series of
questions and answers runs like a thread through
all the texts of the sacred literature, holding them
together like a necklace of precious stones. We may
cite a variety of these questions, beginning with the
Vedas:

I am ignorant; out of my ignorance I ask
the seers for enlightenment.
               R. Veda I.164-6

The Upanishads are structured mostly on the
dialogues between teacher and pupil; for example:

I ask you, of that Being who is to be known
only from the Upanishads, who definitely projects those [all] beings and withdraws them into Himself, and who is at
the same time transcendent.
               Bṛhadāraṇyaka III.9-26

The *Praśnopanisad* is composed of the sustained dialogues between six enlightened seekers

of Truth and the great sage Uddālaka. The *Taittirī-yopanisad* propounds one of the well-known definitions of Brahman, as stated by Varuna in answer to his son's question: "Sir, teach me the knowledge of Brahman."

Taittirīya III. I-I

Other famous conversations may be cited from other Upanishads. [1] When we come to the Epics and Puranas and other auxiliary texts, we meet with the same pattern. The *Mahabharata* comes into being as discourse on *dharma*, propounded by a sage in response to questions from a large concourse of seers, who had assembled to perform the ritual of a fire sacrifice [*yajna*]. The *Ramayana* was composed by the poet-sage Vālmiki in order to answer the question: Can there be a perfect man on earth? Other books on *dharma* are also mainly resolutions of queries regarding righteous conduct in the world or away from the world.

The questioning is important because the teachers, although compassionate, do not feel called upon to interfere with the course of events as it obtains in the world. Reformers do not play a major role in the history of Hinduism, not because the world is perfect but because they are in tune with the primal cosmic rhythm of creation, its sustenance, and also its dissolution. Reforms belong with the world and therefore come under the purview of all men of good will who wish to follow a righteous way of life. The man of knowledge who has penetrated the mystery of creation experiences no disharmony that must be set right. To him all is as it should be and not otherwise. Yet because of his boundless compassion for suffering humanity, he gives of himself and his peace to all who seek.

His way of being in the world is itself a boon for the whole world.

The role of the teacher is to awaken the yearning for the ultimate *desideratum*. By the example of his living presence, he lends support to the message of the scriptures. The scriptures are like road maps of a difficult terrain leading to a marvelous destination. The teacher is the guide who assures the pilgrim that such a goal not only exists in reality but also is attainable by anyone who is prepared to embark on the journey toward it. Many times the worthwhileness of this enterprise is questioned by despairing wayfarers. The teacher instills, as it were, new courage in the seeker and uplifts his flagging spirits. In answer to the question "Wherefore should I engage this arduous task?" the teacher may quote the following text:

> Brahman is Reality, Consciousness and Infinity; he who realizes Him treasured in the cave in the highest space, even as Brahman the omniscient, fulfills all wants at once.
>
> Taittiriyopanisad II.I-I

Realization, indeed, is to attain everything at once, to know the plenum of joy and to be liberated from every alienation. Since man seeks happiness, why should he not pursue a path that would lead him to the perfect joy of a homecoming?

The spiritual journey is undertaken in faith and in the hope of attaining perfect fulfillment. The practical side of the spiritual journey is, therefore, totally God-oriented. Yogic exercises may be undertaken because they help in controlling the mind and containing the senses. Moral excellence is the foundation of religious endeavor. The watchword for a person desirous of leading a spiritual ife is containment or *saṁyama*. Obedience, humility, one-pointedness, truthfulness, abstinence, and such other moral virtues are to be practiced by a devout pilgrim.

The language of seeking and finding indicates the hiddenness of the goal. God is the mystery of all mysteries. He hides Himself so that He may be sought for his own sake and not for anything else. The whole gamut of sacred literature is concentrated on the concealment of the divine source of all being. Just as a curtain hides that which is beyond the curtain (as well as unveiling that which it hides), so the scriptures indicate the presence of the Supreme Being beyond the facade of a multiplicity of religious enterprises. The variegated nature of this multifarious activity could be confusing and uncongenial to the non-Hindu, but within the tradition it serves the purpose of imparting an aura of holiness to all aspects of human life. Nothing in the world is "other" to the presence of God. He is everywhere and eternally so. The seeker needs to do nothing but turn his attention toward whichever aspect of the veil is conducive to his bringing his full faculties to bear on its removal, thus beginning his trek toward his spiritual goal.

The Vedas speak of Brahman as the Ultimate Reality. The impersonal nature of this cosmic reality is personalized as God in many texts. That which is transcendent is also immanent in all creation. Since God has no particular form, He may reveal Himself in any form suited to the occasion. His proximity as the self within the heart of man is a constant theme for all types of sacred literature. The many God images worshipped in the temples and shrines are so many aspects of the same reality. The Vedic Brahman-Ishvara-God became Ráma-Krishna-Śiva-Devi of the later Epics and Puranas. The characterizations of Brahman as stated in the *Taittiriyopanisad are: sat* (reality), *cit* (consciousness), and *ananta* (infinity). These terms do not add up to a definition but are features indicating the nature of Brahman, which is bliss (II.I-I). Thus, the one common term which is used for God is *Saccidananda*—the word *ananta* (infinite) being interchangeable with *ānanda* (bliss) because the plenum of bliss knows no fragmentations.

In order to understand the panoramic vision of Hinduism, one could develop an appreciaton of the eternal shadow play of the real and the unreal which comprise our experience in the world. Hinduism does not seek to neglect the world. In fact, the world is inescapably demanding as a sphere of judgment and action which must be given heed to by all men of good intention. The religious quest for spiritual enlightenment, on the other hand, stirs the imagination of a negligible number. Religion as a way of total commitment to God exercises only a very tenuous influence and that, too, can be easily dispensable. According to Hinduism, God does not demand that his creatures obey Him and turn to Him only in fear and anxiety; He also requires that in their search they perceive Him to be indispensable to their way of being in the world. The word *require* is apt in this context because God's need of man is the sunlight that raises the sap of man's seeking for God.

The world, therefore, is important for Hinduism. It is the indispensable theater of activity where human beings come to grips with their inescapable imperfectibility and also find (if they are desirous of doing so) the all but hidden way toward the attainment of perfection, not beyond death, but here and now. Hinduism, we can say, is squarely rooted in the belief that the world is a veil for the reality of God. The veil is also a reality; otherwise it could not conceal. To the enlightened seer, it is a veil, albeit a colorful and engaging one, whereas to ordinary people it is reality itself.

Time belongs with the world. Beginnings, maintenances, modifications, and annihilations mark the progress of time. Much minunderstanding could be avoided if it could be seen that Hinduism does not deny the kaleidoscopic panorama of the world; in fact, how can one deny something that is an existential reality? On the contrary, attention is focussed on the magnetic nature of the world because it is projected as reality itself. It is important as the takeoff point for a life of inquiry into the ultimate nature of man's own inner being. The vedic vision sees the world as a sphere of forgetfulness. It takes the world seriously as an inescapable arena of overpowering engagements, and therefore man is called upon not to expend himself entirely in it. The seers speak of a mystery that is more worthy of being accepted as a challenge for man's highest faculties. In India somehow this vedic vision has prevailed. The Indian tradition has painstakingly maintained a grip on the subtle pointers to the existence of a reality beyond the world—or rather in spite of the world. Hinduism, we may say, is the long history of a tradition that, rising and ebbing with the tide of time, has had its attention unalterably fixed on the quest of the unknown, yet eminently knowable, region of grace.

CHAPTER TWO

THE DIMENSION OF THE SACRED

India is particularly rich in the possession of sacred literature. The concept of "sacred" in this context is rather wide ranging in its application. As stated earlier, the Hindus believe that the most worthwhile duty of man is the pursuit of the transnatural dimension of human life, which lends meaning to his earthly existence. Whatever acts as an incentive to this quest, or as a reminder of or a perspective on it, is sacred. To raise the everyday ordinary consciousness to the contemplation of the Divine Being [*Brahman*] is the heart of all modes of religious endeavor that have come to prevail in India.

The word *sacred* is used here in opposition to the word *secular*. Of late we have become familiar with many forms of the quest for extra-mundane experience. To seek to raise the power of human consciousness to its upper limits without reference to the yearning for God-realization is to remain within the sphere of the secular. The Hindu, on the other hand, is basically a devout person. The quest for extra-mundane experience is inoperative for the Hindu unless it is based upon a belief in God and man's need of Him. Spiritual practices are meaningful only in the context of a religious way of life.

As we have noted, Hindus use the term *saccidananda* (reality, consciousness, bliss) to express their idea of God.[1] God is reality; He is of the nature of consciousness (that is, not nondynamic and not nonspiritual) and is fulfillment itself, without a trace of shortcoming. His perfection overflows with auspicious qualities. Hindus embrace the idea that the presence of God is not only all-pervasive and ever-abiding but also responsive to invocative prayers. God is, in fact, the nearest of the near *antaryamin*[2], yet He hides Himself so that man may engage in the quest for God-realization. The Hindus, therefore, surround themselves with symbols that evoke God-remembrance. The concept of pervasive sacredness may be compared with the all-enveloping sunlight which shines—especially in a mirror—so that it stands out as a focal point of rare brilliance. Thus the Hindu is devoted to his holy rivers, sacred mountains, and temples that enshrine beloved images of God, and to numerous festivals that celebrate many auspicious moments of divine manifestations.

The intermingling of the dimensions of transcendence and immanence is emphasized repeatedly in Hindu sacred literature. He who in essence is without form assumes countless forms in order that a devotee may find refuge at his feet. The spiritual longings of men in quest of God coalesce and give shape to various images which an artist may concretize in a variety of media—clay, metal, stone, wood, canvas. Sometimes such images are installed in temples with appropriate ceremonies with the help of qualified priests. The installation ceremonies indicate that the presence of God is being invoked in the image. The many images of the Hindu pantheon are not many gods, but are different aspects of the same ultimate reality called *saccidānanda*.

This way of relating to God is peculiar to Hinduism. It may be likened to the various roles a man is required to assume in the world. The same man is father, son, friend, husband, etc. to different people. A son knows about his father's other aspects, but his personal attachment flows along the singular relationship of son to father. This dimension of a personal attachment to God as father, mother, child, beloved, master, or friend explains the meaning of the phrase *iṣṭa devatā. Iṣṭa* may be translated as "personally most desirable" and *devatā* indicated the particular image of God that inspires the devotee to his greatest effort toward spiritual emancipation. The God-image most dear to the heart of a man is his own personal key to the mystery of the divine cosmic panorama that he seeks to unravel. All who worship the same *iṣṭa devatā* become part of a brotherhood [*sampradaya* that develops a separate identity. The many *sampradayas* (traditions) are distinct but not exclusive ways of worship. They are, therefore, more an enrichment than not. The variety of the ways of worship is pleasing to the Hindu because he is not familiar with the concept of regimentation in the sphere of man-God relationship. A channeling of de-

votion along one single idea is foreign to Indian tradition. Man is free to seek God in the way that suits
him best. All divine manifestations are, therefore,
sacred to the Hindu, all houses of God are holy
shrines, and all religions are ways of relating to the
same divine source of man's being.

The freedom to worship many God-images is
based on the thought that there is no exclusive way
to "salvation." Men are born with differing propensities in unequal situations, and they inherit vary-
ing cultural backgrounds. Moreover, human beings
cannot by themselves rise above the sphere of
natural phenomena. It is only through the voice of
the scriptures that man is recalled to a state of
awakening to the possibility of the transnatural
amid the natural. But it is first of all necessary to
arouse his attention so that he can engage his will
toward this quest. Since the quest is the way to freedom, it is appropriate that the protagonist should
have a choice in the matter.

The idea of a choice in the matter of worship
conjures up an image of utter confusion. But just
as the "many" hide the presence of the One Ultimate Being, so the diverse ways of worship constitute one unified condition for the attainment of fulfillment. *Mumukṣutva* is the term for that state of
one-pointed yearning for the knowledge of the ultimate reality, a knowledge that precludes any more
searching or doing. This state of finality is expressed by many terms: self-realization [*ātma-
sākṣātkāra*], liberation [*mukti*], or other equivalent
phrases. As stated earlier, what the theistic
philosopher would call "God-realization" (by way
of *bhakti* or devotion) would be termed "self-
realization" (by way of *jñana* or knowledge) by the
advaitin or nondualist. Both terms indicate a free-

dom from the limited state of mortality. The nuances of philosophic distinctions are not really divisive because all the great pathfinders agree on one point; namely, man's seeking ends with the state of yearning; the finding is an act of grace. The "compassionate teacher" of the *advaitin* is easily identified with a God-image of the devout mind. The many denominations within the fold of Hinduism are not entirely mutually exclusive since they remain united under the heading of *āstika dharma*. The term *āstika* means "those who are determined in their beliefs by the Vedas."

The whole of Hindu sacred literature, then, is absorbed in answering these questions: Why should man seek God? Why should he be required to turn away from the world in order to find Him who is the Creator of this world? How is this turning around equated with bliss itself? All the major scriptures highlight similar questions while engaging in discourses with the interlocutors. The answers to these questions may be summarized in these words: Man seeks God because it is his nature to do so. The union of man and God is the "natural" state of bliss. The world seems to lie like a shadow between the two, creating an illusion of duality when actually man and God are one. The world is also permeated by divine nature because there can be nothing completely "other" to God. In order to focus on the immanence of God, every aspect of human commerce with the world order is brought under the rubric of the sacred. Celebrations like marriage, for example, are primarily religious functions. The bride and groom, as well as the parents, are required to abstain from food until the ceremony is over. Importance is attached to the worship of family deities and the main ritual of the taking of vows is performed in proximity to the sacrificial fire [*yojna*]. Other important events of family life are also invested with an aura of religious festivity: for example, when a baby is given solid food for the first time [*annaprāśana*] or when a child is taught the alphabet [*vidyārambha*].

In Hinduism man's environment is considered to be an extension of his own nature. There is a difference only in degrees of awareness among creatures, man being the highest of all because of his self-awareness. Rocks and stones, trees and bushes, springs and rivers, birds and animals, are all members of the same family, held together by the fact of divine presence pervading and yet transcending the entirety of creation.

The non-Hindu is under the impression that only the cow is sacred in India. It is not generally understood that a host of other creatures are also sacred: apes, snakes, some species of birds. In fact, almost every animal has one day in the year dedicated to its worship—as well as the worship of the deities the animal is associated with. Plants, trees, rivers, and lakes are also remembered and honored in accordance with prescribed rituals on specific dates during the year. Pilgrimages are undertaken to holy sites throughout the year.

In short, life is circumscribed by reminders of the dimension of the sacred. All things are symbolic of the one reality that remains hidden behind the facade of the world. The world as the veil is also sacred. The devout approach the veil with reverence in their hearts because the scriptures say that it is man's duty to seek as best he can and await the descent of divine grace, which is free and spontaneous. One does not know when the auspicious moment will come—when the veil stands dissolved and the seeker finds himself face to face with his heart's most cherished desire. So all is sacred; all is of the divine essence. The more one can be in tune with the cyclic orders of the rhythm of creation and dissolution in nature, the nearer one comes to the center of the mystery of the universe.

The word *sacred*, when applied to entities like a cow, a banyan tree, or a river, denotes the special quality of divine presence in them. The quality of being sacred does not make them singular objects of worship, which would strip the word of its meaning. Just as a man with superior qualities is not to be worshipped as God, so it is with all the other creatures and objects in the scale of creation. The meaning of *sacred* derives from the reverential attitude of the onlooker. Every culture cherishes its own paradigmatic vison of Him who is to be worshipped as the Supreme Being. For Hinduism the ideal has been man's attainment of knowledge of Brahman as bliss.

> He [that is Bhṛgu] came to know Brahman as Bliss; because all this [creation] is born out of Bliss, being born, it is sustained in Bliss; then it moves back toward Bliss and dissolves into Bliss.
>
> Taittiryopanisad III.6

The reality of Brahman pervades everything—to the tiniest blade of grass. To the devout a blade of grass is holy because he sees in it the presence of the divine. To see the panorama of the world as divine play is to live within the scale of the sacred. The quest for eternal joy could, after all, begin only with the experience of the spark of delight in all things. The touch of the delight of Brahman imparts holiness to the entirety of creation. A seeker approaches a sacred object with devotion and in turn clothes the emblem with his own aura of reverence. This reciprocity heightens the awareness of the one and widens the efficacy of the other. Sacredness is another way of looking at this mutuality of reverence and grace.

The way of devotion is slightly different from the way of knowledge. The man who begins by way of discriminating between the real and the nonreal turns away from the shadow world as not worthy of his attention. The turning around of the man of knowledge and the joyful participation of the man of devotion are two aspects of the same quest for celestial joy which is the goal for both. Sometimes the two attitudes are distinguished by saying that the first is the way of philosophy and the second that of religion. The man of religious aspirations seeks to find God in his life; the philosopher seeks to discover the witness-self, who is none other than the "footprint of Brahman" in the innermost cave of his heart.

The Atman within the very texture of man's being helps to unravel the mystery of the cosmic principle, Brahman. By speaking of Atman, the texts promise the accessibility of Brahman. The inadequacy of language causes the use of such words as *proximity, accessibility,* etc. As a matter of fact, Atman is not different from Brahman; the realization of this truth is the supreme gain of perfection.

CHAPTER THREE

THE CLASSIFICATION OF TEXTS: RELIGION AND PHILOSOPHY

Hindu sacred literature can be considered under two broad divisions: 1) that which is heard and memorized [*śruti*], and 2) that which is written or recorded from memory [*smṛti*]. *Śruti* is identified with the more familiar word *Veda*. The Vedas are four in number: *Ṛk, Yajur, Sama,* and *Atharva* and are the ultimate referents for religion as well as philosophy in India.[1] Another pair of terms, *apauruṣeya* and *pauruṣeya,* is sometimes used to make the distinction clear between *śruti* and *smṛti.*

The term *apauruṣeya* is not easily translated into another language. We may begin by saying that Veda is more than the outpouring of the inspired, intuitive knowledge of man. The syllable groups known as *mantra* are symbols for that which they

speak about. They appear as if unbidden like a flash
of lightning suddenly irradiating the understanding of the poets who are already seized by a yearning for Truth.[2] To become aware of the radiant
presence of the ever-abiding reality is to achieve a
state of one-ness with it. The terms *to achieve, the
state,* and *become aware* are inadequate because
language falls short of explicating the bliss of self-
realization, which is said to be fulfillment itself. Enlightenment is an experience which spontaneoul-
sy resolves into paeans of incalculable joy. The utterances indicating the ecstasy of the poet-seer are
also mantras. The entire Vedic corpus thus
prefigures the ultimate mystery of Being because
it speaks of the Truth of Brahman. Without the Vedas, there would be no knowledge of Brahman, so
Brahman is Veda and "to know" the Veda is "to
know" Brahman. To know is to be: *brahmaveda
brahmaiva bhavati* (the knower of Brahman becomes Brahman) (Mundakokpaniṣad 3-2-9).

Veda, therefore, is *apauruṣeya,* the very being
of the ultimate reality, Brahman. The language of
Veda, appropriately, is known as *alaukika* (divine).
Although the letters and words of the mantra
resemble mundane language, in this case, classical Sanskrit, they lie beyond human powers of
creativity by virture of their unique sequence of syllables [*karma*], rhythm [*chhanda*], and cadence
[*svara*]. It is believed by the faithful that this structure abides eternally, lending continuity through
mundane time to the tradition that derives its total sustenance from it.

The meaning of *apauruṣeya* will become more
clear when we consider the bulk of *smṛti* literature,
all of which is known to be *pauruṣeya.* These com-
positons are written in non-vedic Sanskrit and are

thought to be the words of God spoken to worthy recipients. These divine revelations were recorded by great sages themselves or were transmitted to disciples for the guidance of the devout. The compilers begin by saying that they received such knowledge from those who had heard the divine voice directly. Such phrases as "The Lord said" occur for the first time in these texts. The mandates of *smṛti* therefore cannot be disregarded or disputed by individuals on the strength of their conscience. If a discrepancy should occur between two such books, then Veda is to be invoked. The key words for exegesis here are *śraddhā* (reverence) and *samanvaya* (reconciliation). The test of scholarship in India lies in the ability of the speaker or the writer to hold together in harmony the three ways to knowledge; namely, *śruti prasthāna*, *smṛti prasthāna*, and *nyāya prasthāna* (rational argumentation). Under the general rubric of *nyāya* are included the philosophies [*darśana*] of India.

Reason is the inalienable right of man to be himself. If the supernatural region is to be made meaningful to him, then the appeal can only be made through reason. In this context, a crucial difference between "reason" and "reasonable" becomes important. Since no dogma or creed is presented for immediate and total obedience, a reasonable outline of what is truly desirable for man *śreyas* is sufficient for engaging his attention toward it. The cultural background of centuries of such discourses for his ultimate benefit predisposes a Hindu to the hearing of the utterances of the Veda as brought to him through the medium of the *smṛti* and *nyaya* ways of knowledge. It is true that a man in the street has no direct knowledge of the Vedas. But he is entitled to read and study what is known

popularly as the *pancamo veda* (the Fifth Veda),
that is, the eighteen Puranas and the two Epics,
Ramayana and Mahabharata. Nothing that belongs
with the Vedas is left out of these auxiliary orders
of scriptures. The Vedas are exclusive to the highest
caste, but "Veda" is universally available to anyone
who is interested enough to seek to know about
Brahman. Just as ways of seeking can be legion,
so the variety of discourses which cater to this seeking are also countless. The proliferation of literature
on sacred subjects is like the swirls and eddies in
a river. They are inevitable because a strongly flow-
ing stream not only appropriates obstacles, but
rises and swells into a more powerful current in order to do so. The Indian heritage of sacred literature
is added onto in every century because every passing age produces its own order of seekers. This
reciprocity is integral to the relationship which obtains between exclusivity and universality. The Vedas are changeless, but "Veda" recognizes time as
a category of existence.

It is sometimes said that religion and
philosophy are identical in India. This is not entirely
true because philosphy is an open-ended concern.
It grows and expands into well-defined systems supported by arguments defending the thesis being
presented by a scholar. These logically consistent
systems are to a certain extent mutually exclusive
and have remained so for many centuries.
Philosophy is a legitimate concern for rational human beings; reason, being discursive, cannot be
held circumscribed by one point of view. It can be
seen to explore every possibility of meaning and ar-
rive at differing positions of intellectual commit-
ments. These philosophical systems occupy in India the same position as the "many gods" of reli-

gious persuasions. These distinctions enrich the fabric of the cultural heritage. Just as the many god-images enhance the mystery of the one Reality, so the many philosophical points of view are brought under a common soteriology, namely, freedom from bondage to the world. All systems are pathways to the true understanding of the human condition.

The philosophical systems are well defined, although as is usual in India, their origins remain shrouded in mystery. Scholarly investigations put forward the following suggestions regarding authorship and dates of the six orthodox systems:

Satnkhya-Sūtra by Kapila, c. pre-Buddhistic, 7th century B.C.

Yoga-Sūtra by Patanjali, c. Pre-Buddhistic, 7th century B.C.

Nyāya-Sūtra by Gautama, c. 2nd-3rd century B.C.

Vaiśeṣika-Sūtra by Kanāda, c. 2nd-3rd century B.C.

Pūrva-Mimāṁsā-Sūtra by Jaimini, c. 4th century B.C.

Uttara-Mimāṁsā or

The *Brahma-Sūtra* by Badarāyaṇa, c. 4th century B.C.

The legendary names of the originators are recognized as those of the recipients of divine wisdom. The books are written in the form of a series of aphorisms. New orientations in philosophy begin with the decoding, as it were, of the sutras (aphorisms). Systems develop along the lines inaugurated by a great commentator and are taken up for further elucidation by his disciples. Along with the six orthodox systems, the Hindu tradition recognizes three nonorthodox systems, that is, those that do not subscribe to the authority of the Vedas.

These are the Carvaka system, Jainism, and Buddhism.

The Nonorthodox Systems

The Carvakas: The origin of this system is in pre-Buddhistic times. Diffused and pervasive, the system holds an ancient attitude of scepticism regarding the Vedic declarations of the nonnatural dimension of human life. All faithful followers of the vedic traditon had to contend with the Carvakas and defend their position against ruthless criticism. The Carvakas were materialists in their philosophical attitude. They did not believe in an afterlife or in God. They accounted for the principle of consciousness by saying that it is an evolution of nature and that the difference between consciousness and the body is one of degree rather than quality. They rejected out of hand the vedic understanding of the spiritual matrix of the cosmic order. Death was the supreme reality for the Carvakas. Nothing remained after death; life on this earth was to be enjoyed to the full. In order that this enjoyment be pure and lasting, the Carvakas laid down rules of moral conduct to guide society. Thus we find that a secular form of morality without reference to religion has been a familiar concept in India since ancient times.

Jainism: Jainism is the classical ascetic philosophy of India which has a rigorous framework of moral rules for householders as well as those who remove themselves from the world in order to seek liberation. The aim of human life is to free the soul of its bondage to karma. Jainism has a tradition of great enlightened teachers who come into the world in order to help mankind. The teacher for this age is Mahavira, who was a contemporary of Buddha. Both Buddhism and Jainism strongly oppose the vedic sacrifice as being of no religious value. The Buddha taught the way to Nirvana through a progressive order of nonattachment to the world as well as to one's own individuality. Attachments give shape and substance to what we call the human soul. If attachments coud be nullified, then emotional imbalances would also cease to agonize the mind. The cessation of all agitation would bring about a state of utter peace and stillness that is familiarly known as *Nirvana*.

The sixth century B.C. in India saw the rise of these two elaborate nonorthodox systems. Jainism has survived as a vigorous religion and enriches the culture of India by the living examples of many of its saintly men and women. Buddhism, on the other hand, went out of India to flourish in the neighboring regions. It again returned to India in the form of Tantricism and influenced other similar cults prevailing at the time. The intermingling of various religions on the soil of India, giving rise to powerful cults, is in itself a fascinating study. In the proximity of Hinduism the proliferations came as new beginnings or expansions rather than as rejections or radicalizations of the old.

The Orthodox Systems

Sainkhya, Yoga, Mimamsa, and the principles of Nyaya, or argumentation, are the common heritage of the Vedanta philosophy of India. The ontological positions vary and are debated by adherents. This imparts distinctions and exclusivity to the schools, but they all subscribe to the general view of man as heir to his divine heritage of perfection. The philosophical schools that prevail in India at the present moment are based on the Vedanta. Vedanta is another name for the Upanishads,

which form the last part of the Vedas. Sometime
in the beginning of the Sutra period, Badarayana
is believed to have compiled a book of aphorisms
which hold together the teachings of the Upanishads. This book is called the *Brahmasutra* or
the *Vedanta-Sutra*. Another important work came
into existence in the epic age. The Mahabharata
contains the teachings of the Upanishads in the
form of the *Gita*, written as a dialogue between
Krishna and Arjuna.

These three source [*prasthāna-traya*] are the
foundations of Vedanta philosophy; namely, the Upanishads, the Grahma-Sutra, and the Gita. They are
consecutively called the *Śrutiprasthana*, the
Smṛtiprasthana, and the *Nyayaprasthana*. The
three pillars of Vedanta are taken from *Sruti*, *Smṛti*,
and *Darśana* (philosophy). All who wish to be heard
by a company of scholars are required to write commentaries on the three sources. In India all original writings are written in the form of commentaries on the classical material. Sometimes the
author mentions his own name, more often the
name of his own teacher, and most often he chooses
to remain anonymous. The dates and authorship
of many classical works are thus perennial subjects
of controversy in academic circles.

The three source materials of Vedanta have
given rise to a number of philosophies with different positions regarding the nature of ultimate reality. The earliest is the Advaita philosophy of the
eighth and ninth centuries A.D. Commentaries on
the Upanishads, the Gita, and the Brahmasutra
coordinate the teachings of the three and establish
the unity of Brahman and Atman. The individual
self and the world are both nonreal, masquerading
as the real. Enlightenment comes to be when the

of influences of the Agamas, Tantras, Puranas, and Itihasas on each other is hard to disentangle. The methodology of deciphering exact lines of demarcation is not considered a rewarding process in the tradition. The religious way of life has naturally undergone transformations since the vedic times; whatever was feasible and apt at that time made way for such practices as became more suitable later on. What is important here is the nature of the all-pervasive area of influence of the Vedas. They continued to exercise the same influence on the expanding and tangentially developing ways of religious life as one the way of the *yajna* of the vedic times. The Vedas remained the ultimate referrent for all religions. No religion within the fold of Hinduism wished to be outside the pale of the authority of the Vedas or to become *Veda-bāhya*. The strength of the connections varied but even a tenuous one was considered more congenial than to be termed *Vedabahya*.

Philosophy as well as religion in India is structured on the dialogue between those who seek and those who, out of compassion, graciously show the way. Both belong to the order of literature called *pauruṣeya* or *smṛti* or what in commensurable language may be called revealed knowledge by virtue of the mystery of their origin as well as their transnatural concern for the welfare of human beings. It is not at all difficult to see how the Upanishadic reference to the ultimate being as the Indweller [*antaryamin*] in the heart of man became metamorphosed into images of Narayana, Śiva, Durga, Rāma, and Kṛṣṇa of the Puranas and the Epics as the *Iṣṭa-devatā* of the various brotherhoods.

The processes of transformation would be important for relgious consciousness if we could find

corresponding parallels between the quality of significance and the passing of time. This criterion is
singularly held in abeyance in Hinduism. Nothing
is obsolete here, or the newness of a doctrine does
not take away the importance of its message if it
carries with it the mark of "revelation." For example, the two Epics, Ramayana and Mahabharata, (c.
5th century or earlier, B.C.) are fully as authoritative in the tradition as the *Bhagavatpurana*, which
is a late work belonging probably to the tenth century A.D. For such reasons as these, the distinction
between Vedism and Hinduism remains inoperative from the point of view of the orthodox Hindu.

Subsequent chapters contain a more detailed
study of some of the texts mentioned here, beginning with the Vedas.

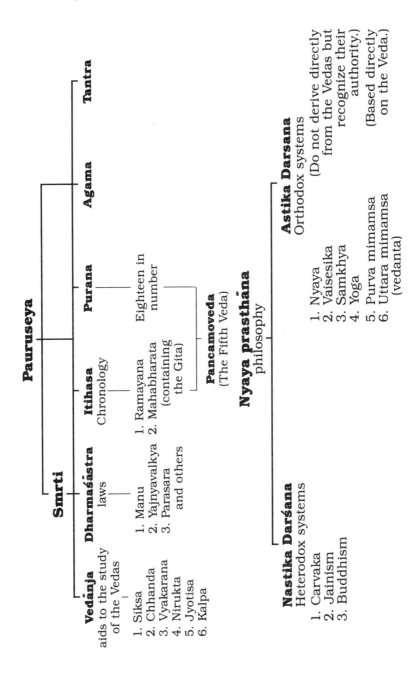

Pauruseya

Smrti

Vedánja
aids to the study
of the Vedas

1. Siksa
2. Chhanda
3. Vyakarana
4. Nirukta
5. Jyotisa
6. Kalpa

Dharmaśastra
laws

1. Manu
2. Yajnyavalkya
3. Parasara
   and others

Itihasa
Chronology

1. Ramayana
2. Mahabharata
   (containing
   the Gita)

Purana

Eighteen in
number

Agama

Tantra

Pancamoveda
(The Fifth Veda)

Nyaya prasthána
philosophy

Nastika Darśana
Heterodox systems

1. Carvaka
2. Jainism
3. Buddhism

Astika Darsana
Orthodox systems

(Do not derive directly
from the Vedas but
recognize their
authority.)

1. Nyaya
2. Vaisesika
3. Samkhya
4. Yoga
5. Purva mimamsa
6. Uttara mimamsa
   (vedanta)

(Based directly
on the Veda.)

CHAPTER FOUR

THE VEDAS

The four Vedas, as available to us today, are collections of hymns, guidelines for rituals, rules of normative conduct, and philosophical discourses regarding the one reality called Brahman. The Vedas were recited and memorized by generations of pupils living in hermitages under the tutelage of seers and enlightened sages. These forest dwellings, *asrama*, were residential seats of learning where young students lived for a number of years until they became well versed in various arts and skills and learnings. Thereafter, they returned to the settlements to take up their respective duties in their communities.

The vedic tradition has lived and survived in the memories of qualified personnel who are spe-

cifically educated for this purpose. These pupils belong to families of Brahmins, the highest caste in
the caste system of India. All Brahmin families inherit particular branches of the Vedas as their own
special field of study. These families are expected
to recite daily these texts [*svadhyaya*] and maintain the tradition by passing on the teachings to the
next generation of youngsters. In our own age this
practice has dwindled to very few families scattered
in some of the cities where vedic studies still survive the impact of uncongenial influences. The
printing and reading of books or their study in
educational institutions are not part of the tradition. The continuity of proper recitation [*svadhyaya*] by those who are qualified to do so is ob-
ligatory in this instance.

It is not by chance that the vedic literature is
still available to us. It is supported by a well-
developed system of memorizing and transmission
to students. There are eight artificial and three
natural modes of arranging the syllables of the
texts, as for example, the first and the third, the second the fourth, and so on. These various orders
ensure that no sequence is lost or extraneous matter interpolated into the text. The methodology of
this process of memorizing in order to preserve the
unity of the entire body of literature, is an exact
science with its ramifications of grammatical rules
and specified rhythms regarding pronunciations.
For this reason, when the Vedas came to be written and transliterated into other languages, a profound unity was seen to uphold the texts recited
from memory by scholars belonging to different
parts of India. This remarkable continuity,
preserved so painstakingly and faithfully by generations of vedic scholars, is for the Hindu a fact of

metaphysical importance, because the Veda is sometimes defined as *Sampradayavicchede sati asmaryamanakartrkatvam.*

This definition may be rendered freely since the vedic heritage is "a continuing, unbroken tradition of self-authenticating literature." The Veda is not subject to proofs because the Veda in itself is the only source of information indicating the vibrant presence of the ultimate reality. The mantras are not brought into being by the seers, but they are self-revealed. In turn the poets transmit this vision as joyous tidings to their disciples. The Hindus believe that the Vedas are eternally present, but they are "recovered" within the scale of time by seers for the guidance of seekers of knowledge.

In our own time the available vedic literature is not complete and parts of it are said to be "lost." Tradition, however, upholds the belief that the Vedas are eternal and can never be lost. Whatever is not manifest in the living memory of man remains unmanifest and hidden in the region of Aditya or the Sun. The Sun is the visible, ever-present sustainer of this creation and the Vedas abide with it till dissolution. They become manifest with creation and remain unmanifest during dissolution. A story is related in a Purana[2] regarding the recovery of Veda from the *saurya-mandala* (the region of the sun) by the seer Yajnyavalkya: Guru Vaisampayana on one occasion was required to perform great penance to expiate some unworthy act committed by him. He gathered his disciples together and asked them to undertake the penance on his behalf jointly so that the burden would not be too great on any one of them. Yajnavalkya, the favorite, stepped forward and said, "There is no need for all of us to do penance. I alone will accomplish it." The teacher was annoyed by the show of arrogance and took away the rights of discipleship from Yajnavalkya. Further, he was asked to "return" all the teachings already imparted to him. Yajnavalkya obediently belched out the entirety of the knowledge acquired by him at the ashram of the Guru. The latter, then, asked his other disciples to assume the bodies of Tittiri birds and eat up the "food" given up by Yajnavalkya. This knowledge give up by Yajnavalkya and saved by Tittiris is known as the Krsna-yajurveda. The sage Yajnavalkya in his turn went away to do severe penance and perform austerities in order to regain the knowledge lost by him. By proper *tapasya* he became Brahmavit (knower of Brahman) by the grace of the great God Savita (the Sun). This knowledge acquired by the sage is known to us as the Sukla-yajurveda.

The story accounts for the two divisions of the Yajurveda and also indicates that Brahman-knowledge is eternally present in the Saurya-mandala. Fragmentation of this eternally abiding truth is with us because we are limited beings. Since truth is homogeneous, even the fragments are considered to be complete in themselves; the Veda, therefore, as available to us is taken to be complete and supreme knowledge itself.

Mantra Samhita

The first part of each Veda is called *samhita*, which comprises hymns to the gods. The worship of many gods is sometimes condemned as thoughtless primitiveness or unphilosophical idol-worship. All primitive cultures have shown a course of development in historical times from worship of many gods to the awareness of one God, a progression from polytheism to monotheism. The Hindu tradition is peculiarly neither polytheistic nor monotheistic. Max Mueller coined a phrase, "henotheism," to fit the case of worship enjoined in the Vedas. Many gods are extolled but each hymn gives the highest praises to the god to which it is dedicated. How can many gods be supreme lords of creation? This supremacy of each god in turn is termed "henotheism." The more natural interpretation with which Hindus are familiar is that the Veda teaches all are manifestations of the same reality. A hymn to a particular god is a hymn to that one reality that remains hidden as the ground of all that is visible, felt, or known to us. Some hymns do not refer to any gods at all, but are addressed to the one reality. The famous Nasadiya Sukta says:

There was neither the nonexistent nor was the existent then; there was neither the region nor the sky that is above. What did cover it? Where, in whose protection? Was there water, unfathomable, deep?

There was neither death, nor immortality. There was not even the distinct knowledge of night and day. That one breathed without wind by its will power, other than that there was nothing beyond.

The darkness was concealed with darkness in the beginning. All this [world] was indistinguishable water. That which existed was covered with all-pervading void; through the power of austerity that one was born.

Desire, that was the first seed of the mind, came upon that in the beginning. The sages, having searched in their heart

with wisdom, found out the bond of existent in the non-existent.

Their [web of effects] was extended
like the ray of the Sun; was it across? Or
was it below? Or was it above? There were
impregnative; there were great forces; food
was below, and consumers [were] above.

Who know truly? Who shall here
proclaim whence it is born? Whence its
vivid creation? Gods are later by the creation of this universe. Then who knows
whence it has come into being?

Whence this vivid creation has come
into being; either he held it or if he did not
[then who held it]? He who is the lord of
this [creation] is in the highest heaven; certainly he knows it; or if he does not know
[then who knows]?

Rkveda .129 1-7[1]

The hymn states that the gods are coterminous
with creation; they are to be worshipped as the first
manifestations of the divine. The vedic culture is
embedded in mythology. It does not seek to emerge
into an air of pure rationality because mythology
itself is considered to be a dimension of truth. Thus,
in the Vedas, the worship of many gods forms the
framework for the meditation on the one reality. The
basic thought of Hinduism that the many are for
the One, runs through all its variety of expressions.

The Brahmanas

Mantras are used as recitations on the occasion
of sacrifices. The second section called brahmanas
are manuals giving guidelines regarding the performance of yajnas. The yajna (sacrifice) lies at the

heart of the vedic tradition. It is a mode of relating to that one overarching and underlying unity which transcends as well as is immanent in all multiplicity. By the mode of oblations consigned to the sacred fires, singing of hymns or adoration, etc., the Hindu established commerce with the gods, who are our elders in the hierarchy of the sportive-creation or *srstilila* of God. In our mundane world, we see clearly that the commerce of give and take upholds the entirety of human relationships. A family, a community, a nation, or even the one world in which we live cannot survive without the reciprocity of self-restraint on the part of one and acceptance on the part of another. He who denies himself in one respect is fulfilled from another quarter. Duties and rights, privileges and obligations are so dovetailed that one loses meaning without the other. This universal law is upheld in the ritual of sacrifice. The rising flames of the fire symbolize the mingling of the two dimensions of reverential worship on the one hand, and benedictory granting of boons on the other. All aspects of human life are permeated by the thought that in anything and in everything one must invoke the presence of the divine. From the birth of a child to the death of an aged one, all are events, strung like pearls on the same thread of the universal rhythm of life and death.

The objective of the vedic seer was to attain a well-balanced life of plenitude and happiness in the world by establishing a harmonious accord with the cosmic powers, visible as well as invisible. The yajna is a community project which deployed all professions practiced at the time. It was also important for welding the family together because husband and wife performed the yajna as a team. The ritual holds together man and nature, as well as the sphere beyond man and nature. Fire also symbolizes the manifestation of the unmanifest. The yajna forms the bridge between the action-filled world and the forest of retirement, between the *karma-kanda* and the *janan-kanda* of the Vedas. To ask for enrichment in worldly goods, *preyas* (that which is pleasing to man) does not stand in opposition to the prayer for enlightenment, *Sreyas* (that which is most desirable for man) because the taste for unalloyed ever-abiding bliss is created by the unsatisfactory nature of the joys of the world. The ritual of yajna keeps alive the intermingling as well as the crucial separation of the regions of action in the world and the insight for penetrating the secret of the world as a veil of reality.

The Aranyakas

After a useful life in the world as a seeker of truth (or a couple together) one could repair to forest hermitages where he (or they) would meditate on such questions as one of perennial interest and hold discourses with other like minded people. This could be a life of retirement, spent in studying and teaching. The forest schools were both for those who were on the threshold of entering society and those who, having discharged their debts to a particular society, were seeking to engage in a greater task for the benefit of the whole of mankind.

In order to get a glilmpse of the society of vedic times, we may cite from the following sermon spoken to the pupils on the eve of their departure from a forest hermitage. The pupils have finished their education and are about to enter society as responsible householders. The very first injunction emphasized by the teacher is: Truth is to be spoken and practiced; no deviation from Truth must take place; righteousness should be cultivated, the pupil should discharge his obligations to his teacher (before entering the world) and also to his family by getting married. Carelessness in anything is not allowable; without being cruel to others, he should observe the right of self-protection; he must discharge all duties of the householder, be specifically respectful toward his mother, his father, and his teacher; the guest is to be honored, all actions which are priaseworthy are to be resorted to but not those of the other kind . . . .

The teacher then propounds a remarkable criterion for ethical judgments. He says, "When in doubt, look around and see how good men of the highest integrity of character, the highly respected Brahmins "who are not cruel" behave, and take your cue from them. Even for "accused people" the same rule holds good. The injunction does not state simply to mete out justice to wrong doers, but again the criterion is to be guided by the judgment of those who are well versed in such matters and who are good and righteous and not cruel, and are desirous of acquiring merit for their actions (deliberations in this case, that is, they will not act in haste) (*Taittiryopanisad I*). Morality here is squarely based upon precept and conscious emulation of the goodness in other worthy leaders of society, rather than one's own evaluation of a situation. In this context we must keep in mind the fact that Brahmins were privileged, not because they had power or wealth, but because they had moral, intellectual, and spiritual excellence, and so were worthy of emulation. A combination of moral excellence together with wealth and power is a rare phenomenon, given due recognition in the character of Janaka, etc., but ordinarily learning, power, wealth, and constructive work were divided up for Brahmins, Ksatriyas, Vaisyas, and Sudras. These were the four castes of Hinduism. A mingling of these privileges makes for disorder in society, but we see that in vedic times, Brahmins were poor scholars engaged in the pursuit of knowledge only and in imparting it to deserving pupils. They had no worldly privileges. They enjoyed a prestigious position in society by virtue of their total commitment to an otherworldly life.

The Upanishads

The Upanishads are the best known of all Hindu sacred literature. Traditionally thirteen upanishads are enumerated as major texts: Ten commented upon by Samkaracarya, two from which he has quoted in his works, and the Svetasvatara. These are as follows:

From the Rgveda—Aitereya and Kausitaki

From Suklka-yajurveda—Isa, Brhadaranyaka

From Krsna-yajurveda—Katha, Taittiriya, Kaivalya, and Svetasvatara

From Samaveda—Kena and Chhandogya

From Atharvaveda—Prasna, Mundaka and Mandukya

All upanishads, however, are equally important as source material for the teaching about the oneness of Brahman and Atman. The lists vary somewhat but in general the number is fixed at 108 as given in the Muktikopanisad. All Upanishads begin with invocatory hymns to gods asking for their blessings and seeking their help for the inquiry into Brahmavidya. The well-known vedic commentator Sayanacarya (14th century A.D.) writes that it is meet that the gods like Mitra, Varuna, etc. should be propitiated by man because by seeking to ac-

quire Brahman-knowledge, he is preparing to for-
sake the region of the influence of the gods. Just
as responsible shepherds guard their flock against
night marauders like tigers, etc., so do the gods seek
to preserve human beings against the possibility
of the transcendence of the human conditon—gods
are sustained by human beings and therefore men
are zealously guarded by their spiritual patrons.
Thus, unless the gods kindly remove such obstacles as may impede the progress of the scholar, he
cannot hope to reach his goal. The invocatory
chants, therefore, indicate that the main thrust of
the texts is toward Brahman-Knowledge alone, by
which man is to proceed on a path unknown to and
unchartered by worldly wisdom.

All upanishads propound the knowledge of the
unity of the Self and Brahman. The Mundakok-
panisad raises and answers this question: What is
that on knowing which everything else may be
known? (I-1-3) Another form of the same question
is:

I ask you, of that Being who is to be known
only from the Upanishads who definitely
projects those [all] beings and withdraws
them into Himself, and who is at the same
time transcendent?
Brhadaranyakokpanisad III.9-26.

The favorite form of answer to such questions
is the paradox, as for example:

That [Brahman] moves; That does not
move. That is far off; That is very near;
That is inside all, and That is outside.
Isopanisad 5.

> It is known to him to whom It is unknown;
> he does not know to whom It is known.
> It is unknown to those who know well, and
> known to those who do not know.
>
> > Kathopanisad II.3

The paradox is used as a breakthrough—to point out that ordinary cognitive language is inadequate in this instance. All statements that indicate the unknowability of Brahman also aim at focussing on its hiddenness:

> The eye does not go there, nor speech, nor mind.
>
> > Kanopanisad I.3

> This Self is not attained through study, nor through the intellect, nor through much hearing.
>
> > Mundokkopanisad III.2.34

Such passages indicate the otherworldly nature of the quest; the calling attention to the yearning for Self-knowledge. Mere curiosity will not unlock the gateway because:

> He is to be attained only by the one whom the [Self] chooses. To such a one the Self reveals His own nature.
>
> > Kathapanisad I.2.23

The specific language expressing one-ness of Self and Brahman is known as a statement of great value—a *mahavakya*. Four such meta-statements are accepted as crucial in the vedic tradition:

1. Prajnanam brahma: Aiteryopanisad 5.3 (Rgveda)
2. Aham brahmasmi: Brhadaranyakopanisad 1.4.10 (Yajur Veda)
3. Tattvamasi: Chhandogyopanisad 6.9.4 (Sama Veda)
4. Ayamatma brahma: Mandukyopanisad 2. (Atharva Veda)

What, then, is the Self and how is it the same as Brahman? Many answers to this question are given in the upanishads. Brahman, who is of the nature of reality, consciousness, infinity (Taittriyopanisad II.1.1) is also of the texture of the bliss matrix itself (Ibid., II.6.1). The same Brahman resides in the cave of the heart well hidden as the innermost Witness-Self, and because of his presence within man, all else is made meaningful to him. The pertinent question here is: "How should one become aware of the Self?" or "Why should 'I' who am not so aware seek to know Brahman?"

An answer to this question is stated in the brhadaranyakopanisad, which has become famous by virtue of the innumerable exegetical works founded upon it. The story which is given twice in the same upanishad (II.iv.1-14) is as follows:

Sage Yajnavalkya on the eve of his departure from home for the life of a renunciate seeks to take permission of his two wives, Katyayani and Maitreyi, and also to divide his worldly goods equally between them. Katyayani is agreeable, but Maitreyi asks: "Sir, if indeed this whole earth full of wealth be mine, shall I be immortal through that?"

"No," replied Yajnavalkya, "your life wil be just like that of people who have plenty of things but there is no hope of immortality through wealth."

Maitreyi thereupon asks to be taught the way to immortality. Yajnavalkya is pleased and speaks to her as follows:

> My dear, you have been my beloved and what you say is after my heart—Come, take your seat, I will explain it to you. As I explain, meditate [on its meaning]. It is not for the sake of the husband, my dear, that he is loved, but for one's own sake that he is loved. It is not for the sake of the wife, my dear, that she is loved, but for one's own sake that she is loved. It is not for the sake of the sons, my dear, that they are loved, but for one's own sake that they are loved. It is not for the sake of wealth, my dear, that it is loved, but for one's own sake that it is loved . . . .)

Yajnavalkya proceeds to enumerate other things and then concludes by saying,

> "The Self [for which all are meaningful in life] my dear Maitreyi, should be realized—should be heard about, reflected on and meditated upon! By the realization of the Self, my dear, through hearing, reflection, and meditation, all is known."

The sage continues to describe the all-inclusive and all-pervasive nature of the Self:

> "As a lump of salt dropped into water dissolves with water and no one is able to pick it up, but from wheresoever one takes

it, it tastes salt, even so, my dear, this great, endless, infinite reality is but Pure Intelligence. [The Self] comes out [as a separate identity] from these elements and [this separateness] is destroyed with them. After attaining [this oneness] it has no more consciousness. This is what I say, my dear."

Maitreyi expresses her doubt by asking how it is possible for the Self to lose consciousness when it attains immortality. To this Yajnavalkya returns the answer that has become the anchor sheet of the Advaita philosophy:

Because when there is duality, as it were, then one smells something, one sees something, one hears something, one speaks something, one thinks something, one knows something. [But] when to the knower of Brahman everything has become the Self, then what should one smell and through what, what should one see and through what, what should one hear and through what, what should one speak and through what, what should one think and through what, what should one know and through what? Through what should one know that owing to which all this is known—through what, O Maitreyi, should one know the *Knower*?

The rhetorical question marks the limit of the intellectual quest. Thereafter the disciple and the teacher enter upon the practical phase of the matter; the spiritual exercises which wil bring about the necessary changes in the way of being of truth. Elsewhere (Taittiriyoponisad) is described the process of the gradual unveiling of the layers of sheaths hiding the Self. The I-consciousness is sought to be detached from its sense of identity with, first the body, then the life-breath, then the mind, intellect, and feeling. When all five false identifications are eliminated, Self-realization takes place. It is not that a new state is achieved—it is rather in the nature of an awakening, a recovery. Veils being dissipated, the Self shines forth as the ever-abiding light by which all else is illuminated—a state of fulfillment that leaves nothing more to be desired and therefore is the achievement of unalloyed bliss without a trace of shortcoming. The following couplet is a favorite quotation with all commentators describing the felicity of ultimate achievement:

Bhidyate hrdayagranthi schhidyante sarvasam sayah ksiyante casya karmani tasmindrste paravare.
Mundokopanisad II.2-8.

The knot of the heart is penetrated, all doubts are resolved, all bondages are destroyed, on seeing Him who is here and beyond.

The Upanishad, therefore, is primarily, for the *sanyasi* or the ascetic who has renounced the world. Renunciation as a concept is easily understood in India, becaue Hindus have lived and breathed the tradition of discrimination between that which is pleasing [*preyas*] and that which is to be preferred [*sreyas*] as an ultimate goal of human life. Renunciation does not mean a physical gesture of disgust with the world. Such an attitude actually would be a bar to renunciation. Renunciation is that state of the mind which is all-consuming yearning for supreme knowledge. It cannot be foretold when one may be inspired by this *jijnasa* and at what age. The Upanishads, therefore, relate the intellectual quests of kings, sages, women (ascetics as well as housewives), men of low birth, and also the very young. The *jnasu* (seeker) is beyond all distinguishing marks.

The teaching of the unity of the self and Brahman is imparted in many ways. In every case the disciple is required to "see" for himself the truth being discoursed upon by a process of meditative austerity [*tapasya*]. On the realization of this truth, the disciple is joyous and in turn becomes a *brahmavit*. The brahmavit, whatever his caste, age or sex is of the community of the ṛṣi. We see, therefore, that this teaching is highly selective and yet completely universal in that anyone may become a *jijnasu* and thus qualify himself as a suitable disciple for the lesson in brahma-vidyā.

It may be asked why a desire to know, coupled with the teachings already available in the Upanishads, should not suffice for self-realization. This brings us to the fact of the indispensability of the teacher (guru) in the tradition. The knower of Brahman may enkindle the light of self-knowledge. A description of a sparkling lamp may be very pleasing but it cannot ignite the fire which is required for lighting other lamps.

There is another aspect to this necessity for the teacher. A man who is in ignorance does not know that he is laboring under a misapprehension. To him the error is truth. It is an outsider who alone can point out the error for him. The nature of this error and enlightenment is related in the following story used very often in philosophical writings as *dasamo'siti* (you are the tenth):

Ten men are obliged to swim across a river at night. Arriving at the other shore, they want to ensure that none is lost. The man who takes a tally omits to include himself and there is great anguish and sorrow at this "loss." A compassionate passerby (although he knows there is no cause for alarm) takes pity on his predicament. He taps the man on the shoulder and says, "You are the tenth." There is great rejoicing at this "recovery."

The human being living in the world is in a state of forgetfulness of his real nature. The gracious teacher helps him to become aware of his state of ignorance. Nothing else needs to be done. Once doubt about what is apparently real but in reality unreal is enkindled, the disciple is set on the road to *jijnasa* regarding the quest for self-knowledge. This turning around from an outward vision to an inner vision is called renunciation.

CHAPTER FIVE

THE SMRITIS

With the genre of smriti literature we enter the juris-
diction of time and can see its influence as a
category of existence. The massive proliferation of
sacred texts seems to have kept pace with the in-
creasing complexities in societies, the many movements of emigrations, and influxes of peoples on
the plains of India. Diverse trends were integrated
and became part of the same homogenous cultural pattern. It is considered unnecessry and even un-
seemly to seek to pick out the individual strands
of this many-colored garment because the insis-
tence on continuity and homogeneity is not without
its metaphysical overtones.

The Overcoming of Time

The belief in cyclic order in time imparts a relativity that is perhaps peculiar to the Indian tradition. The relationship with passing time has been given its full importance in the present century. The possiblity that man is merely a historical being haunts the consciousness of modern man because it means that he in essence is a creature of his time and is determined by the changes that time may bring and his authenticity lies in relating to them meaningfully. This relegation of the power of destiny to time is a modern way of assessing the human condition and belongs with the belief in a linear concept of time, marked by stages of beginings, progressive enlightenment, and finally, a goal which is within the purview of human strivings. Modern man is very conscious of his responsibility toward the world which he seeks to shape in accordance with his own understanding of the fitness of things.

The Hindu takes a slightly oblique stance on this question inasmuch as he can agree with it to a certain degree only. Hindus cannot subscribe to the view that man is nothing but a creature of his time. It is true that time and place are the two most powerful determining factors that shape his way of life in the world. All changes in time are relevant and of supreme moment to anyone who is desirous of understanding the givenness of his earthly existence It would be a truism to say that as long as we live and strive in the world, all time-bound values are true and worthwhile. The role of Hindu sacred literature may be seen as the thin end of the wedge that seeks first to raise doubts in the mind regarding the overwhelming influence of the time-bound world which apparently sets the limits to our understanding.

The vedic tradition does not oppose the world. Discrimination rather than rejection lies at the heart of the Hindu way of life. From the scriptures a man may learn about the true nature of his being, about God, the divine person, on knowing whom all else is known. God is never absent from the heart of man, but he does not know that he entertains this exalted presence within the texture of his being, as it were. How can he be made aware of this ignorance as well as the possibility of the state of blessedness? To this task the scriptures address themselves in a variety of ways. The vedic tradition does not, therefore, trivialize the world, but calls into question its demand to be considered the sole sphere of truth. It seeks to present the world as the dimension of the not-Self, the arena of forgetfulness from whence the Self is to be recalled to the pathway which leads to knowledge.

Many theories regarding the nature of the world are put forward in the sacred books but they are unified in stating its creation by God. The cosmic powers of creation, sustenance, and dissolution are divine and it is not given to man to appropriate them as human. The changes that time brings about in the ways of the world, therefore from the cosmic point of view, are extra-mundane. To omniscience alone can belong the wisdom of legislating for all the stages of progressive time. Creation is divine nature and therefore so is revelation. The simultaneity of transcendence and immanence is the recurring theme of the sacred books of the Hindus which are supposed to be the written records of divine utterances. The coming-to-be of the text is all that matters, whereby God reveals himself in as many ways as his presence may have been invoked by those who desire to know about Him.

According to the legendary history of ancient times, the great sage Vedavyasa wrote the eighteen Puranas and then compiled the Mahabharata. He was aware of the need of the time for an easier access to the vedic lore and made it possible for these texts to manifest themselves through him. In smriti literature God is seen in his various images endowed with an ever majestic, as well as endearing, quality. Smrities, therefore, do not subscribe to the view that men provided these texts as and when need arose for them. Such a view would seem anthropomorphic from the Hindu point of view. Sacred literature is of divine origin and therefore self-authenticating. What is sometimes known as proliferation is better called reiteration of the same theme in language which lay closer to the ordinary usages of it. The age of the *rsi* does not become a thing of the past but is projected onto the passing stages of time in the guise of the continuing dialogues on the subject of liberation.

Hindu scriptures display a close-knit unity of reason and faith. Each text (even the books on law) begins with an inquiry by a worthy disciple who approaches a renowned teacher for enlightenment. Metaphysical discourses forever seek to span the hiatus between the ontology of revelation and the in-depth awareness of the predicament of earthly existence. Thus every age gives rise to its own type of sacred text. It cannot be otherwise because it is divine nature not only to create but also to sustain what is created—sacred literature remains sacred not by virtue of its relevancy according to passing time but because its ever-continuing presence indicates the overcoming of time.

The Texts: *Vedanga*

Ordinarily, the Vedangas are listed first because these pertain to the study of the Vedas. The six Vedangas according to tradition are Siksa (phonetics), Chhandah (metre), Vyakarana (grammar), Nirukta (philosophy), Jkyotisa (astronomy), and Kalpa (exegeses and precepts). The first two deal with the study of the exact enunciation of the vedic texts, the next two are indispensable aids to exegisis, and the last two act as guidelines for the performance of vedic rituals. A vedic scholar is required to be well versed in these studies for a correct understanding of the meaning of the vedic literature.

Dharmasastra

Many law books extant in India are believed to have been written by authors of great antiquity. Traditionally speaking, the laws of Manu are the most important, followed by those of Yajnavalkya and Parasara. Yajnavalkya himself gives a list of twenty other canonical works regarding norms of behavior for the populace. In these works are to be found the details of the structure of Hindu society: the caste system and how it is to be upheld, the details of sacraments, including birth rites, naming ceremonies, marriage rites, and also the last rites of death. Every aspect of life in the world is touched upon and rules are laid down for scrupulous observance.

The Dharma Sastras spell out the four aims of human life. The first three, dharma (righteousness), artha (worldly possessions), and kama (pleasures) pertain to man's worldy existence and the fourth, moksa (liberation) is the supreme goal. It is the veritable apex which alone can impart significance to the other three. According to Manu, "This [moksa] is the highest success for the brahmin who is well versed in the Vedas becaue he attains fulfill-ment thereby and by no other means." (Manusm-riti 12-93)

The Laws as detailed for each section of the community from birth to death are in accordance with the lawgivers' understanding of the vedic mes-sage: It is for human beings to live a life of scrupulous righteousness so that ultimately he may be seized with the yearning for that knowledge which is discoursed upon in the Vedas. Defining dharma, the Yajnavalkya Smriti says:

"Srutih Smrtih sadacarah svasya ca priyamatmanah, Samyaksamkalpajah Kamo dharmamulam idam smrtam."

(I.I.7)

The Sruti, the smriti, the conduct of good men, what appears pleasant to one's own Self, and the desire which springs from a good resolution, are said to be the roots of Dharma, (trans. by S.C. Vasu.)

Dharma is to be derived from a study of the Sruti that is the Vedas, Smritis, or the Laws and also from the lessons derived from the exemplary con-duct of good men. Further, one may decide for one-self regarding options such as when to perform a religious rite, etc., and also such desires spring from decisions made according to the rules of righteous-ness and not self-interest.

The canonical nature of the Laws is undenia-ble, but the Lawgivers wisely made provisions for the inevitable nature of passing ages. Both Manu and Yajnavalkya authorize the forming of legal committees which may be asked to pronounce on such matters as may not be covered by other texts. The constitution of this committee is flexible— ranging from learned brahmins to men who are known to be of good conduct and who are profound scholars. Manusmriti concludes this issue by saying: "Even if thousands of brahmins who have not fulfilled their sacred duties are unacquainted with the Veda and subsist only the name of their caste, meet they cannot form an assembly for settling the sacred law" (12.114).

These lawbooks determine to a large extent the legal system which is extant in India. Ordinarily all sacraments are performed without being reinforced by a parallel secular legal sanction. Legal papers pertaining to births, marriages, and deaths are still a rarity. The religious ceremony performed in accordance with prescribed rules still exercises sufficient binding force to make legal proceedings redundant.

Itihasa and Purana

The Ramayana written by Valmiki and the Mahabharata by Vedavyasa are known as "history" (itihasa) and eighteen lengthy compositions as "ancient legends" (purana) in India. As far as actual dates are concerned, these works are of very little practical help to the modern scholar. Traditionally the statement *pura kale* (in olden times) is enough to situate the stories in the past—exactitude in matters of time remains a non-issue.

The well-defined God-images of Vishu-Narayana, Siva, Sakti, Ganapati, Kartikeya, Rama, and Krishna emerged during the Puranic age. It is difficult to define exact sources and to fix the order of compilations, but for an appreciation of the significance of their religious value, these matters once again may be said to be of no great moment. The religious consciousness of India, it may be said, gave concrete shapes to the vedic gods in the Puranic age. The altars dedicated to them inside the buildings where sacrifices were performed were established permanently within temples.

The most important change brought about was the greater emphasis given to the togetherness of man with God. An involvement with the deity was made possible by an awareness of the object of worship within the scale of human emotions.

The Puranas may be considered the foundation on which Hindu religion has built up its various ideals of theisms. They are repeatedly told tales of God's involvement with his creation, his majesty, his glory, and his compassion and grace, without which man may not achieve the beatitude of God-realization.

If knowledge was the key to the unveiling of Truth during the vedic age, then it could be said that devotion was given greater importance by the compilers of the Itihasas and Puranas. The nearness of man and God was not a new concept; it had already been stated in the Upanishads:

> Two birds that are ever associated and have similar names, cling to the same tree. Of these, the one eats the fruit of divergent tastes, and the other looks on without eating.
>
> Mundakopaniṣad III.1.1

What is new in this age is the mode of relating to God by way of devotion and worship rather than by a concentraiton on the removal of the veils of ignorance. The two modes are the two sides of the same yearning for realization and therefore it may be said that a shift in emphasis alone marks the later ages.

The two "histories" Ramayana and Mahabharata are especially important as introduction to the concept of God's direct participation in the world in a human form. The images of Rama and Krishna are two of the most well-known incarnations of God in India. The concept of incarnations, which is so pervasive in Hindu religious writings, is difficult to explain in other than Indian languages. It belongs with the philosophy of the relationship between God and man. Just as a fowler, or a hunter, entraps his prey by using as decoys birds and beasts of the same species, so does God ensnare human hearts by assuming human forms from time to time.

Not only does He assume human forms for coming among human beings, but also in order to attach the faith, loyalty, and love of his creatures toward Himself. He appears in the image to which they can accord their whole-hearted loving allegiance. God is omniscient and everything is possible with Him but ignorant man may do only his best toward engaging his weak and wavering will toward the quest for knowledge. Any God-image is worthwhile as a point of beginning. To the earnest pilgrim all images are equally awe-inspiring, although his thoughts receive direction and depth when he contemplates the image which is most dear to his heart. This image is his *Iṣṭa-devatā*, the person to whom he can relate in accordance with the requirements of his own unique individuality.

It may be said that in the prsent age the Ramayana and the Mahabharata dominate the religious scene of India. One or the other is read daily almost in every household. Prayers are recited from them. The stories are unfailing sources of inspiration for every art form, literature, dance, drama, music, sculpture, and paintings. Episodes from the earlier epic, the Ramayana, are enacted every year in most cities and villages as a form of celebration of the original advent of the hero Rama. The Ramayana inaugurates the age of classical Sanskrit. It is the first composition to be written in the sixteen-syllable couplet form know as the anuṣṭubha. It is a record of the coming of Ramachandra, his sojourn on earth and his withdrawal from it after completing the task of ridding the world of evil-minded men so that good may prevail once more.

The Mahabhartata is a bigger work; rather, it is a complex compilation of a wide selection of subjects. The central theme is the great war of succession fought between the two houses of the Pandavas and Kauravas. This was a devastating war (c. 12th century B.C.), annihilating thousands of warriors, along with their retinues. The chief protagonist of this epic is King Yudhisthir, who is looked upon as the personification of Dharma (righteousness) on earth. To his aid and support comes Krishna, his cousin, believed by the faithful to be the first true incarnation of the supreme Lord Visnu-Narayana.

The incarnation of Rama is said to be partial because his divinity is hidden behind the exemplary character of his human personality. He is projected by the poet as the ideal son, ideal brother, ideal friend, ideal husband, ideal king and master, and even ideal as the enemy of evil-doers. Rama is the touchstone of perfectability and thus trans-natural in his being, but he is close to the heart of man because he lives, acts, suffers, and rejoices as if he were nothing but a mortal man.

Krishna, on the other hand, is the true incarnation because his aloofness is in close juxtaposition to his involvement with the affairs of his contemporaries. The mystery of his Self-understanding is never penetrated by his people. He is at once with them and yet beyond the grasp of the most enlightened of them. According to the poet seer Vedavyasa, the simultaneity of "togetherness" and "otherness" marks the presence of God on earth.

The two incarnations of Visnu-Narayana as Rama and Krishna hold the hearts and imaginations of all Hindus who belong to the tradition of Vaisnavism; just as Siva belongs with the schools of Saivisms. The Lord as Siva has no incarnations although his descents in some guise or other to the realm of the mundane is celebrated as occasion for the manifestation of his compassion for the faithful.

The entire corpus of the two epics and the eighteen Puranas or legends is devoted to the theme of the intermingling of the dimensions of transcendence and immanence. The overall message seems to be that righteousness or dharma is to be upheld through every vicissitude of life and time; the presence of God is to be invoked constantly so that He may guide the behavior of those who determine the trends of societies. These works provide familiar reading matter to the bulk of the people. They also provide themes for religious discourses which are one of the mediums by which tenets of the faith are imparted to the people. Teaching of the faith is done by the recounting of the examplary behaviors of Rama, Yudhisthira, and other upholders of Dharma.

Hindus, therefore, are familiar with the concept

of divinity as pervasive rather than as completely "other" to man. The aura of all-encompassing mercy as well as wrath was created by the Puranas. The Epics, it may be said,

> "Concretise it into the God-images of Rama and Krishna. In the present century, modern Hindus know themselves as devotees of Rama, Krishna, Siva or Sakti, rather than by their belief in the sanctity of the Vedas. The Vedas, being the privilege of the few, remain closest to the bulk of the people."

The Puranas

The names of the major Puranas as listed in the Matsya Purana are: 1) Padma, 2) Brahma, 3) Vaisnava, 4) Saiva 5) Bhabavata, 6) Naradiya, 7) Markandeya, 8) Agneya, 9) Bhavisya, 10) Brahma vaivarta, 11) Laingama, 12) Varaha, 13) Skanda, 14) Vamanaka, 15) Kaurma, 16) Matsya, 17) Garuda, and 18) Brahmanda

(Matsya Purana LIII, 12-62).

These legends dominate the spiritual ethos of the Hindus and may be looked upon as the background of the Epics. It is perhaps needless to say that there is no chronology here —only a difference in emphasis regarding popularity.

Ordinarily the Puranas deal with five topics: creation, dissolution, transformations as exemplified in genealogies, the descriptive analysis of the timespan of a creation, and narrations about kings and great ascetics. Different Puranas exercise their freedom in dealing with these topics as they prefer.

These teachings are not mere histories, obsolete and pertaining to the past, but they are living ideologies to be perused, meditated upon and exemplified in the lives of people. They are guidelines for living in the world. From this point of view, theories regarding the cosmos, the nature of the world around us, and the lives of heroes as exemplars of the just-life are topics to be cogitated upon and accepted as prescriptive. The Puranic culture is very deep-rooted and pervasive for the Hindu way of life. All aspects of life even today are determined by Puranic concepts and precepts. Doctrines are presented through the medium of narrations. In short, the Puranas in themselves gather up all aspects of Hindu spirituality and present them in a way which could be understood and grasped by the common people. The wisdom of the Vedas and the Agamas have filtered through the Puranas to the level of those who were not eligible for the study of the former.

The teachings contained in the Puranas pertain to the duties of the householder as well as the ascetic; this is why the Puranas are *bhukitmuktipradam*, that is, teacher of the ways of living in the world as well as renunciation leading to ultimate release. Every kind of felicity is vouchsafed to the householder, if he leads a life of good conduct, is devout and righteous in his behavior. The life of *dharma* is taught which itself can lead to *jñāna*, the gateway to moksa, which remains the highest ideal of human life.

The Puranas are devoted to the extolling of the supremacy of various gods. This could be a paradoxical situation. Siva is supreme God in Siva Purana; so is Visnu in Visnu Purana, the Devi in the Devibhagavata. Lord Krishna is stated to be the supreme deity in the Bhagavata Purana. This para-

dox is not without its deeper meaning regarding the
real significance of the way of worship. As stated
earlier, God, indeed, is one without a second, but
He becomes many for his many worshippers.
Whichever form of God is dear to the heart of a devotee, is assumed by Him in his infinite mercy and
compassion for his creatures. He in his innumerable forms becomes the Ista-devata (the beloved) for
the individual seekers of truth. The acosmic conception of Brahman of the Vedas is concretized here
in the various forms of the same *saccidananda*. It
is recognized that in the sphere of spiritual endevor
or *sādhanā*, there can be no regimentation regarding the way of it. Since people are born with vary-
ing predilections, each person must find the most
congenial path for his own capacities. The supreme
reality may be worshipped as Siva, Visnu, Rama,
or Krishna or any other form of God. The Padma
Purana says:

> There is no difference between Siva and
> Visnu. The supreme spirit has only one
> form—We praise Siva in the form of Vis-
> nu and praise Visnu who has the form of
> Siva. Visnu is in Siva's heart and Siva in
> Visnu's heart. (II.71.18-19)

It is stated in the Brahma Purana (56.65) that
Visnu asked Markandeyah to build a temple to Siva.
This was to demonstrate that the two are in reality
the same.

This important concept of the *iṣṭa devatā*
which is so integral to sadhana also makes for the
evolution of distinct brotherhoods, which in the India context are known as *sampradayas*. The line-
age of every sampradaya is long and rich in the pos-

session of specialized modes of relating to the world and also to the sphere of transcendence. Here, we see the emergence of ritualistic worship with its emphasis on mantra-dikṣā or the ceremony of formal initiation into a particular way of worship. Sādhanā or spiriutal endeavor assumes a more personalized form and it inclines towards a greater interiorization. The worshipper is brought very close to his deity in the way he is required to concentrate his mind and fix his attention so that he is wholly absorbed in the object of his adoration. The heart of this system of worship lies in learning to become godlike in order to realize God in one's innermost being.

Festivals and pilgrimages

All Puranas describe in great detail the sanctity of places of pilgrimages. The glorification or *mahatmya* of sacred rivers, mountians, and sites is an important subject in the Puranas. God is everywhere and in everything, yet He is especially present in some places and His presence is easily evoked at particular times. The worshipful adoration with which pilgrims for centuries have congregated at a special site, makes it a vibrant and living source of peace and joy. Alternately, the Puranas themselves are the *tirthas* (place of pilgrimage). It is believed by the devout that the recital of Puranas confers on the hearer not only all felicities pertaining to his life, but ultimately liberation from bondage to the world.

A life of dharma is a life of happiness and contentment. Thus we see that a dharmic life is marked by the observance of many celebrations and festivities. All festivals are commemorative celebrations of great moments of spiritual significance. They also lend unity and cohesion to religious practices and keep alive the traditions sacred to a sampradaya.

Polytheism

The emergence of numerous deities in the spiritual horizon of the vedic religion has led some scholars to distinguish between vedism and Hinduism. The one supreme Brahman seems to have proliferated into many gods. This interpretation is unknown within the tradition. Hindus believe that the same Brahman appears as many. In the vedic times also gods were invoked on various asupicious occasions. They were invoked by uttering mantras and their propitiation or worship was also done with the help of the uttered mantra. The chanting of the mantra was the mode of puja (worship) in earlier times.

In Puranic times we see the worship of images in temples with the help of flowers and fruits,etc. The mode of worship is more concrete and closer to the way of life of the people. The rarefied atmosphere of the yajna, where the utterance of the mantra was the highest form of spiritual communication with the divine, is replace by the mode of puja (worship) and a waiting upon the grace of God for spiritual felicity. There is a difference in degree in awareness and in approach here, rather than a difference in the quality of worship.

The Pancayatana

In the age of the Puranas we see a close linking of the various aspects of the same divine presence in the modes of worship. At least five great gods (sometimes six) are to be invoked and worshipped before any major ceremonial festivity is commenced. This is also the rule for daily worship at home or at temples. All worships are begun with a prayer to Ganesa. Surya, Siva, Devi, and Narayana are the other four deities, who are called upon to bless the undertaking and grant it success. These five are the most popular composite, called the Pancayatana. Sometimes it is augmented by Agni (Agnipurana 327.13; Naradapurana II.41.29.59; Brahmavaivarta II.4.35-36; iv.101.9-10, etc.)

The Puranas fulfill the requirements of the people in changing times and environments of social organizations by filtering the spiritual message of the Hindus without allowing a vacuum to be created or without a break in the continuity of the vedic tradition. The Puranas, therefore, form an important link in the spiritual tradition of India.

CHAPTER SIX

AGAMA AND TANTRA

Agama and Tantra are brought under the rubric of Smriti to specify their essential characteristic of being written by sages who "remember" the words of God spoken to divine interlocutors and are themselves the worthy recipients of the message of these dialogues. Agama and Tantra are distinct from the vedic corpus, but are not outside the area of its influence. Because of the oral nature of the Agamas and Tantras many scholars see a difference in quality between the vedic and agamic traditions. It is true that certain texts oppose the Vedas and so are *Veda-bahya* (outside the pole of vedic influence). These could be counted along with Buddhistic or Jaina Agamas. The Hindu Agamas fall mainly into two groups, *Vaisnava* and *Saiva*. The Shakti-

agamas belong with the Saiva tradition. Some Agamas pertaining to other deities do not oppose these
main trends.

The antiquity, exclusivity, profundity, and
sheer number of these texts make the task of writ-
ing a few pages about them rather absurd. Most of
the Agamas are still not easily available to the reading public, and all of them are to be studied with
a knowledgeable teacher to avoid misunderstand-
ings. Under these circumstances a simplification
alone is possible and it is hoped that no serious vio-
lation is thereby committed.

In a sense the Agamas are more important to
the life of the people than are the Vedas now. Human understanding in confrontation with the impersonal vastness of Brahman is overwhelmed by
a sense of insignificance and incompatibility. The
Agamas brought the cosmic Brahman within reach
of the devotee by giving Him a form and endowing
Him with all the auspicious qualities of beauty,
splendor, and grace. Brahman remains always the
ultimate *sreyas* for the entirety of sacred literature,
bot to God as Visnu-Narayana or as Siva the Hindu may offer his prayers and bring to His worship
love and adoration from the depths of his heart. To
a Hindu the worship of Visnu or Siva as Supreme
God is not an anomalous position. In the words of
a poet:

Mahesvare   va   jagatamdhisvare
janardane va jagadantaratmani dvayor-
na bheda pratipattirasti me tathapi
bhaktistarundrasekhare

(I see no difference between the great
Lord [Siva], the ruler of the entire

universe, and the Supreme Being [Nraya-
ma] who is the soul of the universe but
yet my devotion goes to Him [Siva] who
has the young moon on his crown.
Bhartrihari Vairagyasatakar

It is said the tradition of Hinduism rests upon
four pillars, Sruti, Smriti, Purana, and Agama. The
word *Agama* is also used as a synonym for Tantra.
In this context many authorities can be marshalled
to demonstrate the inner unity of these prasthanas
or foundations. The most well-known quotation in
this regard comes from the commentary of Kulluka Bhatta on Manusmriti: "Sruti is of two kinds,
Vaidiki and Tantriki" (Manusmriti II.1) Kulluka
Bhatta quotes from the Hareeta Samhita and en-
dorses this view.[1] Another well-known text says:

The Veda and the Agama are the true reve-
lations of God. One is general and the
other special with particular reference to
Saivism. Both are His words. Some say
that the ultimate end of these two differ.
But to the great there is no difference.
Tirumantiram C—5th century A.D.
Verse 2397.

According to some Indian scholars, the great
consolidator of Hinduism, the *adi* (first) Samkaracarya, wrote a book on Tantrism just in order
to bring this body of literature its due prominence
as sacred texts. [2] The orthodox view accepts his
authorship of the mystic poetic work *Saundaryala-
hari* (Wave of Beauty) in which he pays homage to
the Goddess Uma. If such indeed is the case, then
Samkaracarya's sponsorship of Tantra and Agama

is a very revealing perspective on this issue, because due to his monistic views, he is the one common protagonist for all teachers who have built up their systems of theologies around the concept of God as supreme reality.

Religions are inescapably monotheistic. Theological exegeses regarding the unity, duality, trinity, or even plurality of the final ontological position does not overshadow the demand for spiritual commitment to the one supreme being. Religions propound the sovereignty of God over his creation. He is immanent as the Self [*antaryamin*] in human beings, and also at the same time, transcendent and beyond ordinary understanding which is determined by cognitive structures. The two major religions of India are Vaisnavism and Saivism. Although the origins of both (historically speaking) may be traced back to pre-Buddhistic eras, their systematic formulation began around the tenth century A.D. in South India. Both gave prominence ot other than Vedic texts and so made their exegetical writings more broad-based.

Vaisnavism

The credit for propounding the first systematic theology is given to the saint of Sri Rangam, Sri Ramanujacarya (c. 11th century A.D.). His writings take into account the Upanishads, the Brahma Sutra, the Gita, the Visnu-purana, the Bhagavat-purana, and works of the same nature. He acknowledges the creative work in this field of his predecessor and teacher, Sri Yamaunacarya. The Vaisnava agamas known as the Pancaratragamas are given the same status, as far as authority is concerned, as the Vedas. Another source, which is equally important, is the collection of sacred hymns by the Alvars. The Alvars were poets inspired by divine love, who roamed at will around the countryside visiting temples and holy sites. There are said to have been twelve such saints, including one woman; the collection of these utterances is called *Divya-Prabandha* (Divine Songs). The worship of Visnu-Naraayana as supreme God became a well-defined *sampradaya* (brotherhood) after Ramanuja. He gave a coordinated form to the diffused trends which pervaded the spiritual consciousness of India. Ramanjua was followed by other teachers of Vaisnavism, who formulated distinct systems, emphasizing philosophical differences regarding the relationship of God, man, and the world. Other brotherhoods which gained prominence were:

Bhedavada (Dualism) of Madhvacarya
(1199-1278 A.D.)
Dvaitadvaita (Dualistic Monism) of Nimbarkacarya (11th century, A.D.)
Shuddhadvaita (Pure Monism) of Ballabhacarya (1473-1531 A.D.)

The same sources (excluding the songs of the saints in the native language) were authoritative for all these teachers of Vaisnavism. Nimbarkacarya and Ballabhacarya gave recognition to the Brindavan-leela of Krishna, the Incarnation of Visnu. They extolled the exploits of the Child-God or Gopal Krishna over that of the speaker of the Gita.

Metaphysics

If we leave out the doctrinal differences, Vaisnavism could be viewed as a religion of devotion, a recognition of the innate difference between the creator and the created. The Brahman of the Up-

anishads could be called acosmic, as interpreted by
Samkaracarya—whatever is, is Brahman. This
monism was repudiated sharply by Sri Ramanuja
and the other Vaisnava teachers. Brahman as God
has the cosmic powers of creator, sustainer, and an-
nihilator. He keeps Himself hidden but reveals Himself to the worthy creature who has surrendered
himself totally and looks to nothing but divine grace
for this salvation. God is the repository of all auspicious qualities like beauty, lovability, splendor, compassion, etc. Within man, he has placed a spark of
his own divinity, so that man may be moved by the
yearning for God-realization.

The relationship between God, man, and the
world is a matter of theological disputation. The
"otherness" of God is subscribed to by all theists,
although the nature of this "otherness" is not the
same. The modes of Sadhana also differ somewhat,
although it will not be wrong to say that all Vaisnava schools believe that it is for man to live a life
of righteousness on earth and engage in devotional practices so that he may prepare himself for salvation. Salvation for the devotee lies in attaining to
the state of proximity or affinity, as it were, with the
Adored One.

The one-ness of Atman and Brahman was criti-
cized by all the Vaisnava teachers as a pernicious
doctrine. The saccidananda image of God, they
maintained, could not be dissolved into the form-
less, quality-less acosmism of monism. To the dis-
cerning and appreciative scholar, this entire debate
regarding the opposition of monism to monotheism indicates the mystery of divine presence, which
remains the ultimate paradox of the one and the
many, the transcendent and the immanent, the creator and the destroyer, the nearest of the near and

yet beyond the grasp of the most intelligent. It is possible to see that the debate could end at the crucial point of deliverance. The monistic theory advances "Hearing of the Mahavakya alone" as the ultimate cause for liberation. This is actually no cause because it is seen to "happen" freely and cannot be brought about by any means whatsoever. The state of yearning [*mumuksatva*] is the limit to which man may bring himself and then await the coming of the compassionate teacher.

> *brahmanyuparatasanto nirindhana*
> *ivanalah ahetukadayesindhuband-*
> *huranamatam satam.*

> Withdrawing himself into Brahman, he [the guru] is ever at peace; he is like a smoldering fire unfed by fuel. He is the ocean of compassion that asks for no reason. He is friend to the pure who make obedience to him.
>
> Vivikacudamani 35

In Vaisnava Sastra the same stage of preparedness is attained by surrendering fully at the feet of God. Grace is pervasive; creation itself is an act of grace. To become aware of this grace in one's life is to become aware of the presence of God here and beyond.

Saivism
During the same time span, the worship of Siva as a supreme God came to be well established in many parts of India. The formative influences are many and their antiquity lies beyond speculative history. Supportive texts are cited from the Vedas.

Many of the Upanishads, such as the Svetasvatara and the Atharvasiras, are of significance in Saivism. Among the Puranas, the Siva-Malapurana is a basic text. The Suta Samhita of the Skanda Purana is also a major source of inspiration. The main determinants, however, are the Agamas or the Tantras, each text being a prasthana (foundation) by itself. There is also a scholarly exegesis on the Brahmasutra by Sri Kantha (contemporary of Sri Ramanujacarya), which puts forward the idea of the supremacy of Siva as Brahman. Thus the link with the Vedic tradition also is forged directly by this commentary.

If commensurable language is permitted, then Saivism comes closest to being what may be called a revealed religion. Siva himself discloses the secret of his nature to worthy recipients. These utterances are Agamas or Tantras. Many criteria are extant for classifying these sacred books. The norm that is the simplest is given here.

Saivagamas may be classified into *vama* (extreme), *daksina* (middle), anmd *siddhanta* (right point of view) (Purvakaranagama 26. 58-61). The extreme section names three other divisions—namely,, Kapala, Kalamukha, and Aghora. The middle range of Agamas are canonical works for what is also known as Trika, Spanda, and Pratyavijna sastra. Some of these texts are: Vijianabhairavagama, Mrgendragama, Malinivijayatantra, Svacchandatantra, and Netra Agama. The crucial text for this tradition, however, is the Siva-sutra compiled by Vasugupta (c. 8th to 9th century A.D.). Many accounts are given regarding the revelation of these aphorisms to Vasugupta by Lord Siva himself. Following directions, Vasugupta is said to have found them inscribed on a stone. Since the site of this revelation was Kashmir, the tradition acquired a regional name.

Much of the fame of this school of thought rests on the work called Isvara-Prateyavijna by Utpaladeva (9th century A.D.). Utpaldeva's teacher, Somananda, was the disciple of Vasugupta; hence the tradition grew by virtue of a teacher-disciple relationship. In the history of the development of this school, the high water mark was reached by Abhinavagupta (c. 999-1015 A.D.). His commentary on the Pratyavijnavimarsini and his other original writings, such as the Tantraloka, are treatises of unparalleled competence on the subject. Abhinavagupta has classified ninety-two Agamas into three groups, according to the ontology that is stated in them. Ten Agamas speak in terms of a dualism; eighteen maintain a position of identity-in-difference; and there are sixty-four texts that establish a nondual monotheism (Tantraloka, Part I).

The third division of our classification is named Saiva Siddhanta, and it is the Saivism that prevails in South India. Twenty-eight Agamas are acceptable to Siddhanta as special to their own tradition. Of these, the first ten are called Bhairavagamas, and the other eighteen are the Rauravagamas.

Revelation is one of the divine characteristics. It is brought forth spontaneously along with creation. The unmanifest utter stillness that is Siva is simultaneously hidden and also expressed as revelation by Sakti; she is the palpable dynamic aspect of Siva. She manifests herself in creation. Agama and Tantra are the indicators of this event of coming-to-be and also of reabsorption into the primal state of dynamic stillness that is visualized by the devotee as Siva and Sakti.

Just as the lifeblood of bhakti was poured into

the veins of Vaisnavism by the inspired poetry of
the Alvars, a similar phenomenon took place with
regard to Saiva Siddhanta also. The formative time
for the worship of Siva as a religion was the age of
the sixty-three saints who lived in the Tamil-
speaking regions over the span of a few centuries
(c. 3rd-10th). Of these *nayanmars* or *adiyars*, as
they are called, Appar, Tirujnanasambandhar, Sun-
daramurti, and Manikkavacakar are the foremost.
After the passing away of the saints, their thoughts
were systematized by teachers who wrote treatises with philosophical import. Of these Meykandadeva, Arunandi-sivacarya, Marai-jnana-sambandha,
and Umapati Sivacarya are known to the blazers
of the trail. Meykandadeva's *Sivajnanabodham*
(13th century A.D.) is the most important text,
which is sometimes compared to Badarayana's
Brahma-sutras of the vedic tradition.[3]

Metaphysics of the Agama and Tantra Sastra

The Upanishads taught the way of discrimination between the Self and the not-Self. By concen-
trating on the areas of the not-Self, the veils of maya
were to be penetrated one by one from the most
gross—the identity with the body as "I" and
"mine"—to the most subtle of intellectual ideations
which, by seeming to correspond closely with the
objective world, appear realistic but nevertheless
emanate from within and also are of the region of
not-Self. That which is completely nonrelational
and yet not-altogether beyond cognition [*na hi
ekantena avisaya*] [*Brahsutrabhasya by Samkaracarya, adhyasa bhasya*] and shines by its own
light is the Self. An elaborate process of inwardization is prescribed, which is of the nature of a
catalyst; that is, after destroying the veil. The

process is also nonexistent, as it were. An inadequate example would be the vanishing of an antidote after it has destroyed poison. The Upanishadic message is: The knower of Brahman becomes Brahman (Mundokopanisad).

The Agamic tradition, it may be said, is an elaboration of the term "becomes" in the above text. The becoming, which was of the nature of "as if" in the Upanishads, becomes real and a spiritual process of divinization. In reality there is not a difference here but a distinct way of looking at the same process of inwardization. The Agamas use a language of separation and reunion rather than a recovery of self-identity. Siva-Sakti are not two but one reality. Siva is unmanifest; Sakti is the entirety of the manifestation as well as the cause of it. The display of her infinte powers is truly a magnificent panorama. This sportive activity is a facade which distracts human beings from thoughts of the unmanifest reality that remains hidden. Spiritual exercises awaken the propensities that create a desire to know the why and wherefore of human existence. The Sastras speak to the seeker of knowledge in terms of the desirability of knowing Siva. The goal of spiritual exercises would lie in attaining the state where the devotee feels the presence of God not only in his inner being but also everywhere.

Tantrasastras give a similar account of the splendid performance of Sakti. Sakti is not a female deity but She is the supreme Goddess by whom all creation is brought into existence, sustained, and withdrawn at the end of time. She is the ultimate repository of the entire potentiality of the created world. The Tantras speak of a descending order of cascading sound movements that become manifest as syllable forms and words with their corresponding objects in the world. The unmanifest is the *paravak*, the ultimate state of subtle vibrant movements that is not caused by anything else because it *is* the primal movement. The preliminary urge toward materialization results in the sound-form called *pasyanti*; the meaning and sound thereof are in union, and the objecthood is not distinct from its energizing power. When the two begin to separate, the Sakti is said to have gained the stage of *madhyama*. Words and their meaning-objects are separated. Lastly, when the words are in ordinary usage in their multifarious forms, the process becomes known as *baikhari*, as it is vocalized in ordinary sound-forms.

To seek to understand the descent and ascent of the Logos or the all-transcending Word is to follow the way of Tantra-sadhana. For the devotee, the Sastras provide the mystic syllable-forms that are symbolic expressions of divinity. Spiritual exercise consists of penetrating the mystery of this separation as well as the union of Siva and Sakti. Every human being is a temple for the deity in his heart. An awakening is followd by Sadhana, to be crowned by a state of realization. As stated elsewhere, the exact delineation of the state of realization is neither possible nor necessary because each pilgrim finds his own answer to his quest. Since sadhana is a way of life for the devotee, the Sastra in every case must make way for the enlightened teacher. The "quality" of enlightenment is homogenous: "The fulfillment of tantra-sadhana is Siva-sadhana, which is indistinguishable from Brahman-realization."[4]

The transformation of the upanishadic quest for Self-knowledge into the devotional commitment toward God-realization is truly a phenomenon of magnificent proportions. The region of that which is unknown but eminently knowable did not become any the less mysterious, yet somehow it seemed more easily approachable to people who had lost the art of holding easy commerce with gods. The passage of time is calculated in ages in India. Every act of creation is divided into the four stages of Satya, Treta, Dvapara, and Kali. Every age is governed by a different set of the sacred texts because the wherewithal of the spiritual journey in some form or other is made available to the pilgrims.

The Mahanirvana Tantra says:

"Sruti is for the age of Satya; Smriti for the age of Treta; Dvapara is to be ruled by the Puranas, and for Kali is prescribed the Agamas only"   (I.28).

The Satya yuga was the age of the naturally good and upright people, prone toward dharma and abstaining easily from evil deeds. This was the age of the Vedas. In the second age of Treta, righteousness is already on the wane. This is the age of the incarnation of Rama, who, by living a life of exemplary goodness, upheld the preponderance of good over evil. The third age of dvapara is fully under the spell of the coming age of evil, the fourth age of Kali. Dvapara is blessed by the advent of Drishna, God incarnate, to guide the affairs of men who are desirous of living the just way of life. An incarnation has been promised for the age of Kali by the Puranas as well; an incarnation that will conquer evil and inaugurate the coming age of truthfulness.

These divisions are fluid. All the characteristics of the four ages are present simultaneously; the difference lies in emphasis only. It is more difficult in the age of Kali to be good and righteous than it was in the previous ages. Human beings are prone to evil propensities and incapable of performing the austerities and leading disciplined lives, which was more the norm in the age of Satya. The Goddess, in her compassion for weak-minded humanity, prayed to her Lord for special scriptures for the age of Kali:

> Under cyclic influence men will natural-
> ly become evil-minded and will be addict-
> ed to sinful acts. O Saviour of the humble!
> O lord! Graciously tell me the means by
> which men may acquire long life, health,
> strength, vigor, and manliness; by which
> they may become learned and sound-
> minded . . . by which men may become
> knowers of Brahman, learned in Brah-
> mavidya (the transcendental science), and
> thinkers on Brahman. I pray thee to tell
> me the means by which their welfare both
> here and hereafter may be secured.
>   Trans. by B.K. Majumdar,
>   Mahanirvana Tantra, First Ullasa.)

The gradual change in emphasis from the way of *tapasya* (austerity) and *jnana* (knowledge) to *karma* (worship) and *bhakti* (devotion) may be com-pared to the building of a mansion that is added onto by every generation of the family. The genius of the architect lies in creating greater accommo-dation without spoiling the facade of the original house. In the Indian context we see the portals of the vedic tradition remaining untouched, but more accessible gateways are added onto from time to time. There have been pseudo-architects who have sought to lay down tortuous modes of ingress into the mansion, but the pristine purity of the original creation is always there to delight the traveler. Time itself destroys what is unworthy and not integral to it.

Only he who is the perceiver of Truth (seer), that is, the enlightened One or an incarnation, a personfication of the descent of grace, can be the spokesman for Sastra or sacred literature. As written above, sacred literature is not manmade. Hindu tradition believes in the possibility of God's participation in human affairs—not only once, but many times, as many times as it may become necessary. The Lord has promised:

"In every age, whenver righteousness is on the wane and evil in ascendancy, I incarnate myself in order to save the devout and punish the evil-minded and to securely establish righteousness"
(Bhagavad Gita 4.7-8).

Such being the background of the spiritual atmosphere, the gradual emergence of various religions as many distinct ways of worship became an integral part of the tradition of Hinduism. Moreover, this mode of expansion is an ongoing process in India and not peculiar to any particular age. A phenomenon has taken place in the last few centuries comparable in magnitude to a previous phenomenon. India is celebrating this year the 500th year of the advent of Sri Gauranga, who had preached to the common people the universal lesson on one-pointed love for God— a love that is un-demanding,unselfish, given freely, because the Beloved is worshipped for his sake alone and for any gain. To the lover Love itself is the supreme gain. Lord Gauranga presented to the people an exemplar who had lived this dimension of love in the previous age of Dvapara, that is, Sri Radha, the heroine of the leela (sportive display) of Brindavan, the birthplace of Krishna. The magnificent array of scholarly theological texts that presents this aspect of Radha ss the inseparable but distinct Sakti of Krishna was composed after the fifteenth century by the disciples of the "lovelorn ascetic" of Navadyeepa (Gauranga). The texts, such as the *Chaitanya Bhagavata* or *Chaitanyacaritamrta*, are religious books of equivalent authority with other Puranas. In our contemporary era, modern Vaisnava *sampradayas* (brotherhoods) pay homage to Radha. Her image is to be found on the same pedestal in every temple dedicated to Krishna. She has so pervaded the religious consciousness of India that to trace the origin of the sanctifying process of this deity would be less than a relevant issue. Yet the acaryas who had pioneered the Vaisnava religion had not mentioned Radha. In fact, this phase of worship was not well know in the ninth or tenth centuries. Love as the crowning achievement of the way of bhakti was established most distinctively by Sri Gauranga, who is believed by the devout to be an incarnation for the age of Kali. Love as the fith *purusartha* (the aim of life) was added to the list of four by him.

It may be explained thus that what men had overlooked as major episodes in the life of Krishna, He himself drew attention to by coming among them once more. At least the romantic imagination of the poet devotees of Bengal was caught by the leela of young Krishna rather than the other aspects of his advent on earth. The devotees do not consider that the recognition given to Radha could be anything but a divine act of grace—a showing of the way to the poorly equipped people of Kali—the way of self-surrender in love. To love oneself, to love the things of the world, is natural to a human being. He lives in this dimension of *kama*—pleasure in objects attained. The way shown by Gauranga is how to transform this *kama* into *prema*—love for God, a love that is fulfillment itself. And how should this be achieved? By singing the beauteous name of Krishna. The name itself will grant the wherewithal of spiritual sustenance to the devout pilgrim.

No fault can be found with any reader who may be confused by the religious panorama presented to him in this little volume. The world is mirrored in Hinduism, and it cannot be reduced to a simple order. Each person is required to face the confusion of life and work out a pattern for himself. What is reiterated in the scriptures again and again is that the quest is worthwhile and the ultimate gain is more than all the heart or mind can imagine, contemplate, or desire.

CHAPTER SEVEN

THE NATURE OF MAN ACCORDING TO HINDUISM

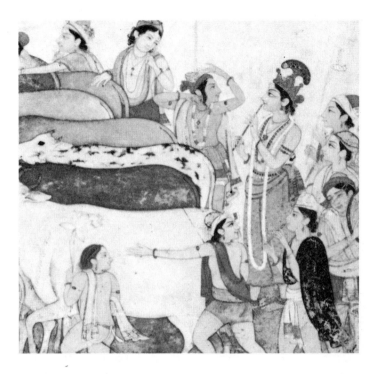

The emphasis in Indian thought is clearly on the man in search of Truth. As far as each individual seeker is concerned, the ontological question central to each system is also to be considered from his own point of view and resolved in the light of the understanding of the word of the scriptures. The authority of the scriptures is supreme, but this authority rests on the alliance of faith, reason, and obedience. The scriptures are to be heard, interiorized by contemplation, and then "lived" by a man desirous of supreme felicity. Intelligibility [*upapatti*] in the light of reason is recognized as a legitimate demand on the part of the seeker of knowledge. Rational as man is, whatever more he may also be, Truth cannot be less than rational or remain forever beyond the corroboration of direct apprehension. So in the ultimate analysis Truth is to be experienced directly and so it is stated by all the authorities (Pancadasi VII 23-27).

How shall we understand man's way of life in the world whence the quest for salvation is to begin? The first things that strikes us is that a definition of man in terms of the usual *pergenus at differentia* does not suffice. In view of the complex nature of the *definiendum*, the definition of man as a rational animal, even if logically cogent, will always remain a too narrow definition. The best that could be done, perhaps, is to list a descriptive series of paradoxes. For example, although man obviously and by nature is a social being, as often as not he seeks solitude (not to escape society, but to be alone with himself); although he must have a lot of pleasurable experiences, too soon he has a revulsion of feeling, again not after satiation, but in the midst of enjoyment; he talks of equality but he would like to preserve at almost any cost his singularity and individuality; we hear of scientists who are devout and also of lay people who find the question of God meaningless because of the discoveries of science; we are not unfamiliar with rationalists who are passionately committed to reason and mystics who are able to describe their experience in sober, rational language.

This list of paradoxes could easily be extended. What emerges is the picture of a being never satisfied with what is, but always concerned with the question of what might be or even what ought to be. Most human lives are spun out in constant oscillation from one to the other. This is not to say that the "is" is not accepted sometimes as a value in itself. It is not the polarity that needs to be stressed, but the fact that evaluation of our situation is endemic to human nature. The systems and structures may change, but the questioning of all that obtains at a given point in time remains an ongoing process.

The Self or "I" for whom this question is meaningful is located somewhere in the psychophysical complex which is the total personality of man. According to some, the Self has its being only in its agency; that is, it is known only in action. Others believe that the essence is in thinking, and yet others emphasize emotional or ecstatic awareness as the clue to the true identity of the Self. However this may be, it is hardly realistic to separate will, awareness, and thought; action, passion, and contemplation; creativity, vision, and insight. Thought is not static. In contemplation we change imperceptibly and become a little like the object we contemplate; in willing or creativity are incorporated vast realms of thought processes; on the other hand, there is no thinking or willing in a vacuum, so to speak. An awareness which is satisfying becomes the incentive for regulating thought or action. In this constantly shifting, dynamic, psychical process, where should we locate the Self?

To come to this question from another angle: Each man is situated in his own particular existential milieu. What is given is the environment in which we participate by acting and reacting to it. We erect for ourselves a world of values that is meaningful for us. Each person lives inside a thought-castle, as it were. Experience and evaluation, action and thought intermingle, succeed, and determine each other constantly—this is our own world of personal relationships. Nobody escapes it. Even if one were to retire to a monastery, one's

thoughts would continue to determine one's behavior. A man is what he is by virtue of what he
believes in and the way he acts upon his belief.

Now it so happens that sometimes this castle
of meaning or significance crumbles partially or totally. Anything may act as a catalyst that dissolves
the carefully built protection around us—a sudden
"transvaluation of values" which throws up the
question "Who am I?" in all its stark urgency. It
cannot be said that this moment of lucidity is al-
way assessed as such by all human beings. It may
come and then be overcome again by the forces of
the world around us, leaving a mood of nostalgia
for a strange world glimpsed as if in a dream.

Since this questioning lies in the vicinity of the
region of grace, why are we not able to abide in it
for any appreciable length of time? Especially as
the scriptures keep on reiterating the supreme
worthwhileness of this quest? The texts proclaim
with great certainty the exalted status of man, albeit not as he is but as he might be. A *de facto* difference is stated between his essence and his existence. It is his destiny to supercede his human condition. Yet, as we live our lives, the gap between the
human and the divine does seem to be absolute.

The crucial point, then, it would seem, is how
man should transform himself so that he can hope
to stay with the quest for spiritual fulfillment. In
other words, let us examine the question of the
separation of man's essence and existence. It is
perhaps well known that Indian thought in general subscribes to the view of the Samkhya system
with regard to the creation of the world and all that
there is in it. The primal source is called *Prakriti*,
the repository of the basic three elements of
creation—*sattva, rajas,* and *tamas.* These are

known as qualities or *gunas*. *Sattva* is the source of lightness, illumination, buoyancy of spirit, joy, serenity, etc. *Tamas* is the opposite quality of heaviness, darkness, sloth, obstruction, apathy, etc. *Rajas* signifies the energizing quality that activates both—it supplies movement, excitement, exhilaration, etc. The three strands are held in a perfect state of equilibrium before creation. The world order is an unfoldment into complexities of the original three qualities and their infinite ways of combinations and permutations. The quiescent stage of *prakriti* is dynamic. Many points of view are advanced as to why this original state of equilibrium is disturbed. For our purposes here we need not take into account the theologies regarding first cause (especially as they are variations on the same idea)—only that once equilibrium is upset—*Sattva* becomes prominent as the first evolute because that is light and buoyant. This is the dimension of the intellect, the most pure in the scale of evolution. Thereupon other stages are reached, such as the I-consciousness, the sensations, and the subtle elements which transform into the material objects of these sensations.

All things are a co-mingling of these three qualities. The nature of a thing is determined by the predominant *guna* in its compositon. A stone is predominantly of the quality of *tamas* and *sattva*. Human beings differ according to the elements of *sattva* and *tamas* in their natures. An apathetic, negative attitude denotes *tamas*, a light, cheerful, happy disposition denotes the presence of *sattva* in an abundant degree. The quality of *rajas* is to be seen in very active people who are capable of experiencing great excitement and who can be very joyous as well as greatly anguished.

Human beings behave in accordance with their nature and behavior in turn formulates further the dispositons that result in activity. The crux of the notion is this: This nature is of the stuff of matter; it is malleable; it can be improved upon; it is the nonessential that fills our horizon and keeps us away from the essential question of the Self that resides well hidden within the "cave of the heart." If and when *sattva* in our nature predominates, then we can stay permanently and not fleetingly with the question "Who am I?" We may then look for the guidance of the scriptures. In fact, the asking of the question already presages the coming of the compassionate teacher because in the ultimate analysis the Self knows itself.

It is not of the essence of the Self to dwell forever in the world as if experiencing joys and sorrows. At times, therefore, human beings are seized with longings for an abiding state of happiness. This "longing" must be carefully distinguished from the wishes and wants a man may have and also see fulfilled in his life.

The variations in temperament are not fortuitous but strictly in accordance with how the material is handled by the person concerned. This is known as the law of karma, which accounts for the difference in aptitude, that is, *adhikari bheda* (difference in eligibility). Karma and eligibility go together. The law of karma is to be understood as an instrument of freedom in the hands of man. What greater power can one enjoy than the freedom to effect changes in the very texture of our nature and destiny. But this power is not unlimited—it operates within the realm of influence of *Prakriti* only. It's greatest achievement is to bring about a predominance of *sattva* in one's nature so that the spiritual yearning is felt. Human nature is already transcended with the asking of the queston, "Who am I" So the moment of alienation from the alien world is nothing but the grace of God. Self-realization, therefore, is God's grace rather than fulfillment of human ambition for transcendence.

The human condition, according to the Hindu tradition, therefore, is preeminently a happy conditon. It is happiness indeed to be born a human being because one may attain God's grace in this life. God dwells in man as his innermost Self. He catches glimpses of this presence now and then in moments of turning around from the world. The Self is the footprint of the supreme reality (Brihaderanyakopanisad I.4-7).

What stands out clearly here is the fact that purusit of what is considered the highest value in life must come as free choice. Salvation is for he who seeks God's grace in life. To pray to God in sorrow or to take refuge at his feet in distress is of spiritual value, but the highest ideal is to seek God for himself only and not for anything else. In the language of the mystics, it is called "falling in love." The lover says to the beloved, "You are my one and only concern." Certainly not less than this is required of the man in search of God. This state of mind is not a conditon of rejection of the world. Just as a human lover has his interest centered on one person, similarly the pilgrim is preoccupied with finding a way for himself. It is quite conceivable that he may even be leading a full and active life in the world, but from the perspective of his ultimate commitment, the world is now insubstantial and shadowy where he goes through the motions of participation without self-involvement. This can be called the mood of detachment *vairagya*, which is indispensable as an item of the wherewithal of a spiritual journey.

The figure of a lover in the secular world is that of an admired hero of countless books and dramas in numberless languages of the world. The figure of the ascetic in total self-surrender to God and in search of his high destiny is equally pleasing to the Indian mind. The ascetic is the idea; man—a man who by his calling is confirming what the books have to say about the ultimately worthwhile quest (*sreyas*) of human life. He is the exemplar because he is trying to bring abut a radical change in the quality of human stuff, in the very texture of our being.

By an ascetic, we do not mean a man in saffron clothes. An ascetic is he who is living the question about his Self. The questioning is being empha-sized because the answer is inevitably related to it. To seek is to find such a man, who then becomes an asset to the world. People may recognize him as a man of wisdom and call him a saint.

The Role of the Saint

A saint may be recognized by his humility and his tranquility. He is at peace with himself and with the world. He is simply an onlooker and makes no proclamations or exhortations. He knows that the world is as God has made it and he does not abrogate to himself any special powers to improve upon it. He is in tune with the cosmic scheme of things; if he is called upon to expound, he may do so, but he may also be content to abide in solitude. He does not seek to change the world, but only to render help to those who are in need of it. The saint's tranquility and affirmation is not the inert-ness of matter but rather the dynamic point of stillness, which balances to a nicety the boundless compassion for suffering humanity and a joyous acceptance of the divine order of things. These ascetics are, therefore, the compassionate ones who as living examples concretize for us the message of the scriptures:

> I know the Supreme Person of Sunlike Color [luster] beyond the darkness. Only by knowing Him does one pass over death. There is no other path for going there.
>
> Sveta Svatara III.8

NOTES

Chapter One

1. Between the god of death, Yama, and the young boy Naciketā (Kaṭhopaniṣad I f.); between Uddalaka and his son Śvetketu (Chhandogyopanisad VI.1-16); between Maitreyi and her husband (Brhadāraṇyakopaniṣad II.4-14).

Chapter Two

1. Saccidanandavigraha, Muktikopaniṣad 1.4; Saccitsukhatmaka, 2.19; ibid, Ramam Vande saccidanandarupam. Ramottasopaniṣad 92., tasmadidam sama saccidanandamayam param brahma.

2. From the scripture a man may have a conception of Brahman as existence, consciousness

and bliss,but he cannot have a direct knowledge of Brahman unless Brahman is recognized as the inner witness in his own personality. Swami Swahananda translation.

Chapter Three

1. Sometimes questions are raised regarding the authenticity of the fourth Veda, but tradition accepts its validity along with that of the other three.
2. Rk. 10.71.3.

Chapter Four

1. The vedic texts were made available to the English-speaking world for the first time at Oxford, England during the year 1849. They were edited by Max Mueller. Since then other editions have been published in French and German.
2. Visnu-purana, III, 5.
3. Translation by N.K.S. Telang and B.B. Chaubey, *The New Vedic Selections* (Bharatiya Vidya Prakashan, 1981), pp. 477-491.
4. These words indicate the necessity for spiritual practices and moral disciplines, in fact, a life of total commitment to the quest.

Chapter Five

1. Incarnation is possible only with God. The re-birth of a human soul belongs completely to a different order of existence.
2. Umapati Sivacarya, *Tisuvarutpayan), v. 45.

Chapter Six

1. Swami Karapatriji of our own times, who was universally recognized as a spokesman for Hin-

duism, also had spoken to support this judgment. Agama Visesanka (Sanmarga, Varanasi), p. 7.

2. Swami Nandanandanananda Saraswati, *Agama Visesanka* (Sanmarg, Varanasi), p. 21. (In Hindi.)

3. K.M. Balasubramanian,, *Special Lectures on Saiva Siddhanta* (Annamatas University, 1954), p. 4.

4. M.N. Sarkar, *Light of Tantra* (Calcutta: Tantrer alo, in Bengali, 1954), p. 3.